# Rhodesian Rid

CW00493814

# Vol. 2

## Dog Training for your grown-up Rhodesian Ridgeback

How to build up a unique relationship with your Rhodesian Ridgeback, using training methods which are tailor-made for your Rhodesian Ridgeback

**©2020, Claudia Kaiser**

**Published by Expertengruppe Verlag**

The contents of this book have been written with great care. However, we cannot guarantee the accuracy, comprehensiveness and topicality of the subject matter. The contents of the book represent the personal experiences and opinions of the author. No legal responsibility or liability will be accepted for damages caused by counter-productive practices or errors of the reader. There is also no guarantee of success. The author, therefore, does not accept responsibility for lack of success, using the methods described in this book.

All information contained herein is purely for information purposes. It does not represent a recommendation or application of the methods mentioned within. This book does not purport to be complete, nor can the topicality and accuracy of the book be guaranteed. This book in no way replaces the competent recommendations of, or care given by a dog school. The author and publisher do not take responsibility for inconvenience or damages caused by use of the information contained herein.

# Rhodesian Ridgeback Training

# Vol. 2

**Dog Training for your grown-up Rhodesian Ridgeback**

How to build up a unique relationship with your Rhodesian Ridgeback, using training methods which are tailor-made for your Rhodesian Ridgeback

Published by Expertengruppe Verlag

# TABLE OF CONTENTS

# ABOUT THE AUTHOR

Claudia Kaiser lives with her husband and dogs Danny (2 years old) and Daika (8 years old), in an old farm-house in beautiful Rhineland, Germany.

At first only as a dog owner, but later and after 20 years actively training dogs, she has gained a lot of experience, helping other people to train their Rhodesian Ridgebacks. She formed the idea of writing this book in order to reach more people, than she could have in the local dog training schools and the small circle of dog owners to whom she gave personal coaching.

The publishing of this guide book is the fruit of considerable research, writing and editing. It is designed to be a guide for all budding Rhodesian Ridgeback owners, to help them get the difficult task of training right the first time, and to avoid those mistakes, which Claudia herself made at the beginning. She worked through her own bad experiences over the years, so that the reader does not have to.

Those who follow the tips and tricks covered in this guidebook are sure to have many years of pleasure from these unusual and wonderful companions.

# PREFACE

Congratulations, you probably made the excellent choice of welcoming a Rhodesian Ridgeback into your life some time ago. You have also recently chosen to buy this guidebook. I would say, you have already made two good decisions.

Your Rhodesian Ridgeback belongs to one of the most outstanding breeds of dog and he deserves to be challenged and supported his whole life long. Only a fully engaged dog leads a really happy and balanced life.

Before you read the next pages, you should know what to expect. This guidebook will not show you any shortcuts to success. Most importantly, reading this book alone will not change anything. Your success depends solely on you.

This guidebook will show you why it is important not to finish the training at the end of puppy school. It will show you how you can train and develop your adult dog his whole life long. Just like humans, dogs continue to develop if we give them the opportunity.

This guidebook will introduce you to many methods which you can carry out by yourself, without help from the dog school. You only need the will and possibly a few utensils for support. It is very simple and practical for everyone. However, I would like to add at this point, that particularly less experienced owners might want to consider an accompanying training at a dog school.

My question to you is now: Are you prepared to invest a few minutes each day – and I mean EVERY day – to make your dog's life more interesting and challenging?

If the answer is yes, then you have made an excellent choice, buying this book. Since you have made the third good choice, you are now ready to read the following pages.

It is very important to me that you are successful in your training. Because of that I would like to mention: Reading this book cannot replace the close working relationship with a personal dog trainer. Dog training relies on a certain amount of finesse. If this is your first dog or if you have a very challenging one, that could have behavioural issues, I recommend taking on board a dog trainer. You will learn a great deal from this book but there is one thing which I cannot offer: That a professional will be watching you during training and is able to give you tips on how you can do it better. Often, you will not notice that something is not quite right.

For everyone else, particularly for experienced owners who are looking for new inspiration, I have no concerns about recommending this book to you without dog school or trainer.

From my heart, I wish you both much success and good luck.

## - Chapter 1 -

# WHAT IS DOG TRAINING?

I assume that, because you have bought this book, you will have been thinking about what dog training is. Usually, people think of two concepts. On the one hand, there is the basic training of the dog, obeying commands such as "sit", "lie down" and "leave". On the other hand, many people associate dog training with a strict, regular training scheme, carried out at a dog school, with a certificate at the end to prove it.

Of course, both variations fall under the category "dog training", but for me it means something different. Firstly, for me, comes the basic training or puppy training and then the full training. But this is not all there is to know. At some point, your Rhodesian Ridgeback will no longer be a puppy and hopefully has mastered his basic training, but not every dog receives further training after that. Not every dog needs it and not every owner has the time or the inclination to do that.

It is more important that there should be a middle way. This is what I call dog training. You may be asking yourself how this dog training, as I call it, is different from the other forms.

Contrary to the basic training, which mostly takes place at puppy age, this training is meant for adult dogs, but presupposes that the dogs participating have received their full basic training. Much of what they will learn here is built on what they already know. This training will not involve learning commands or routines which are important for everyday life and the coexistence of human and animal. This training is not designed to follow a higher goal but is meant to occupy your dog and intensify the relationship between dog and owner.

This is the major difference from traditional dog-school training, where a higher goal is pursued. As already mentioned, this is not the goal here.

At the end there will be no examination and no courses which your dog must take. The training will be relaxed and flexible and you will be able to integrate it into the everyday life of yourself and your Rhodesian Ridgeback.

It is important to note that this is not the only way of training your dog. There are several different types of training which can vary from breed to breed and dog to dog.

Generally, dog training is divided into two categories: "physical training" and "intelligence training", as it is called. Depending on the breed, a dog may prefer the one or the other type of training. Like humans, dogs can show preferences or tendencies which are different from those which you would expect from its breed. For example, a dog which you would expect to prefer physical training may in fact prefer intelligence training. Because of this, I will show you both types of training for your Rhodesian Ridgeback in this book.

At the end of the book I have included a special chapter which covers a very special type of training: "Fun training", which is dear to my heart. Quite honestly, no dog really needs to learn the commands of that training but – and again quite honestly – it is just a lot of fun to train these nonsensical commands. I am sure that it is not just me who has a lot of fun with them, but also my four-legged friends.

I am very proud when my little darlings perform their little tricks.

Now you know what dog training really is and which three types of dog training you can learn in this book. In the next chapter you will learn why it makes so much sense to train your dog and how much it will enrich both your lives.

**The most important facts for you and your Rhodesian Ridgeback at a glance:**

1. The training of your dog is not finished with the basic training, i.e. "sit", "lie down" and "leave".
2. Dog training serves to occupy your dog and build up the relationship between you and your Rhodesian Ridgeback.
3. There is not only one type of dog training. In this guidebook you will learn about physical, intelligence and fun training.
4. Discover in the following chapters which form of training is best for you both. It is important to accept that your Rhodesian Ridgeback is an individual. It is quite possible that your dog does not have so much fun with the type of training which is typical for his breed.

## - Chapter 2 -

# WHY IS DOG TRAINING USEFUL FOR YOUR ADULT RHODESIAN RIDGEBACK?

In contrast to earlier times, today, most dogs are not used as working animals but are kept as family pets. What does that mean for your Rhodesian Ridgeback?

In the past, he had a purpose and was faced with new challenges every day, which he had to solve. He was often not only physically but also mentally challenged and he always knew what he had to do. He was ready for his hunter round the clock. It was expected that he obeys commands immediately but was also capable of acting independently if it were necessary. A lot was expected of a good hound.

These days it is different. The classical hound of those days is now seen as a simple companion in the family and often does not have any duties to perform. No great demands are made of him except that he be well-behaved and little more is expected of him but that he lies still and give his paw from time to time.

This leads unavoidably to your dog being strongly underchallenged, which can lead to behavioural disorders. It means that many Rhodesian Ridgebacks are unbalanced, can sometimes be aggressive (for example towards the furniture) or become hyperactive when their owners return home in the evenings.

I also had to experience this. My first dog - I admit I was very young and had little time – was the sweetest thing. But whenever I left him alone for a longer period of time, he began to rip my home apart. In addition, he tended to be very possessive and did not like others to be close to me.

I did not realise that it was my fault. After all, I loved my rascal and showed him that regularly through intensive waves of affection and mostly extensive walks, mornings and evenings. He attended puppy school and knew the most important commands. We also spent nearly all the time I was at home together, considering he also followed me from room to room.

I was sure that the dog was getting enough exercise and attention. I thought I had done my part. I told myself that it was just bad luck to get a slightly disturbed dog, although this did not in any way reduce my love for him.

However, now I know that it was me and not the dog who was to blame. I had chosen a type of dog which, over the centuries, had been used to working for its living.

Of course, he got enough exercise but that was all. I believed that a little exercise, a little affection and my closeness was completely sufficient for him. But just like us humans, dogs can also suffer from boredom. I know how irritable I can be when I am bored. It is no wonder that my dog behaved as he did.

At that time, I was lucky enough to have been introduced to a dog trainer by a friend. I explained my situation and the problems which I saw in my dog and I asked him for tips on how to change my dog. What was his reaction? He laughed heartily at first, then told me that it was not my dog which had to change completely. I have to admit, that I was confused at first and also a little insulted. However, as I already mentioned, he was a very good trainer and he immediately explained the background to my problems and this is what I want to do for you.

We dog owners in modern times tend to see our dogs either as a piece of sport equipment that will animate us daily to walk outside the front door, or as a cuddly toy which is always ready to receive a stroke from us. The modern dog must always remain still, never attract attention and behave beautifully in restaurants or with friends.

What we have forgotten, though, is that we did not buy a cuddly toy, but a living creature with his own needs. He is not a robot which starts off when we press a button and lies still in the corner of the room when he is not required. This living creature needs to be occupied and not to be a passive part of our lives.

So, what did I change in my everyday life? I still take walks twice a day with my dog but have added 2 training sessions to our daily ritual. Once I realised that I was dealing with a clever dog, I started focusing the training on intelligence games and, because it is so entertaining, also fun training. I changed the content of the walks. We do not just walk beside each other through the woods, I also integrated active interaction which I will tell you about later in the book.

And what did that change?

Everything! I noticed immediately that my dog was much more contented. Yes, I even noticed that he was much more exhausted after just 15 minutes of intensive training than he was after a two-hour walk.

However, what turned out to be much better and really surprised me was the deep and profound bond that we had developed towards each other. We now had a common hobby and we both learned how much fun we can have with each other when we do something together. It was only after this type of training that I could say that my dog was a "friend for life". Before that, he was more a "companion for life".

If you have now realised that your dog is a companion for life and not an active part of it with his own contribution, it is not a bad thing. As I said before, this is the situation with the majority of dog owners.

The difference is that you now have the possibility to change that. You can find out how to do that in the following chapters. But first we have to clarify what you need to beware of in your dog training. There are basic principles and then there are those specific to breed, which need to be taken into consideration. Your Rhodesian Ridgeback must already have had his basic training, without that you cannot continue with this.

**The most important facts for you and your Rhodesian Ridgeback at a quick glance:**

1. Your Rhodesian Ridgeback is a challenging animal which was bred for physical and mental tasks.
2. A Rhodesian Ridgeback, which is only kept as a pet, is in danger of becoming bored and permanently underchallenged, which can quickly turn into destructive energy.
3. Do not just treat your Rhodesian Ridgeback as a passive companion but integrate him actively in your everyday life.
4. Your Rhodesian Ridgeback needs more than just physical exercise because he is much too clever for that. Make him work every day with his head as well as his muscles and allow yourself to be convinced by the results.

- Chapter 3 -

# WHAT SHOULD YOU PAY PARTICULAR ATTENTION TO?

## WHAT IS PARTICULARLY IMPORTANT FOR YOUR RHODESIAN RIDGEBACK?

You have made the conscious decision to buy a Rhodesian Ridgeback. You probably already looked into the various characteristics of different breeds. You will probably already know most of what is to follow. However, because it is so important for your mutual training, I would like to repeat it.

You have chosen the Rhodesian Ridgeback, a breed which is known above all for its even-tempered, alert and friendly character. Although he was originally bred for hunting – he was used against lions and for big game hunting – he is also known as being a family pet.

With a height of 25 to 27 inches to the withers and a weight of 66 to 80 pounds, he belongs to the group of large dogs. His fur is short and red wheaten or wheaten coloured. His most prominent feature is to be found on his back and also has to do with his fur. The hair crest along his backbone grows the opposite way to the rest of his fur. This is why he is called a "Ridgeback".

In Germany, he is not often used for hunting, where his main job was to pin down the wild animals until the hunter arrived. He is more often used as a rescue or police dog.

Enthusiasts love the Rhodesian Ridgeback most for his loyalty and love for his owners. He tends to be more reserved towards strangers. He gets on very well with children and is very patient. For you as the owner, it is important to know that your Rhodesian Ridgeback can be very stubborn. But do not worry, with loving strictness and consistent training you can also get his stubbornness under control.

The strong temperament and healthy self-confidence of the Rhodesian Ridgeback shows itself in dangerous situations when his protective qualities are prominent and he is always ready to protect his territory and the people he loves. He is a very good watchdog, who keeps a very watchful eye on his territory. Unwanted intrusions are met with his deep bark, which he seldom uses without reason.

As you have chosen a historical hunting dog, you should be aware of what that means for your life with him. This four-legged friend is a big energy bundle. The hunting instinct of this breed is very pronounced and you need to be prepared in case he chases cats and wild animals.

If the Rhodesian Ridgeback is not fully occupied, physically and/or mentally, he will tend to become nervous and hyperactive, which could turn into destructiveness towards your furniture. Therefore, plan enough time into your daily routine to keep him busy.

This sensitive and quiet breed is extremely suitable as a family pet. He will never be aggressive and will follow the members of his pack everywhere. In addition, he loves attention and likes to lie at your feet or on your lap – if you let him.

It is important to mention here, that Rhodesian Ridgebacks are in no way suited to living in pens. It is important for him to be integrated into family life and, wherever possible, close to his pack. The quiet nature of the Rhodesian Ridgeback will enable you to take him with you into the office or on journeys.

You will notice, that you have accepted a very challenging dog into your life, but one with huge potential. If you are sporty, you can combine that easily with the needs of your Rhodesian Ridgeback. If you like to solve puzzles or set yourself mental challenges, you will love to do the intelligence training with your dog, and you will notice how much he loves it.

Your Rhodesian Ridgeback will be equipped with all the important components to enable him to enjoy both physical and intelligence training.

Your Rhodesian Ridgeback will generally show a strong hunting instinct. Therefore, you should consider whether you want to satisfy this instinct through retrieval games or dog-dangler training. There is nothing to say against it and it can be very effective. Remember, though, that it triggers the natural hunting instinct of your dog. If this could be a problem for you, you should not continue that type of training.

Of course, I will give you some tips on how to control the hunting instinct caused by retrieval games and dog dangler exercises. This means that he will continue to enjoy hunting – nothing can change that – but that you can control it, which is very valuable. For this reason, you should still read the chapter about that and decide for yourself how you want to proceed.

Although there is a risk of encouraging the hunting instinct of your Rhodesian Ridgeback, the tips will give you the great advantage that he will not chase wild animals or cats.

There are no risks involved in intelligence or fun training for your Rhodesian Ridgeback. The main thing here is to find out what he likes to do best.

**In summary, this means:**

The Rhodesian Ridgeback is a dog for which all three types of training described in this book are suitable. My tip is, therefore, read all three parts and decide afterwards which type of training you would like to start with.

## WHAT TO WATCH OUT FOR?

With dog training, it is not only important to find a type of training which is suitable for the innate characteristics of your dog. It is even more important that both you and your dog enjoy it. If you have found a type of training which your four-legged friend loves, but which cannot motivate you, that is not a good solution. So, listen to your heart as to whether a particular type of training is enjoyable to you too.

If you are not motivated during training, I can already guarantee you, that you will pass that onto your Rhodesian Ridgeback. That makes the training boring for your dog and neither of you will look forward to the next training session. This would undoubtedly lead to disaffection for the training and at some point, you will not want to continue it. Choose a type of training which both of you love. If you are enthusiastic about it, you will almost certainly pass that onto your dog, even if his breed-typical characteristics do not fit perfectly.

Apart from having fun during training, you should ensure that it is physically suitable for your dog. I am sure you have seen dogs which are completely fixated on their balls? The one which jumps in the air for happiness and animates his owner to throw the ball, so that he can dash after it. Do you know of such situations? A dog like that would never dream of finishing the training from himself, even if he is exhausted. He is more likely to have a circulatory collapse than to stop playing. It is important that you know the limitations of your Rhodesian Ridgeback and finish the training early enough to prevent physical or mental exhaustion. This can happen during any form of training.

Keep an eye on your Rhodesian Ridgeback and get a feeling for when he is reaching his limit.

It is possible that some dogs could have problems with training which they love and which is suitable for their breed. I am thinking, for example, of a Border Collie, which is a very active breed and which normally loves agility training. The innate pleasure that this intensive dog sport gives could, if carried out daily, lead to an exercise addiction, which demands increasingly more from your dog.

As often in life, the right balance is important. As strange as it may sound, it is recommended that a physically active dog should focus on more intellectually challenging training. Or in the opposite case, it could be preferable to give physically active training to a more quiet, lethargic dog.

Try to encourage, not only the strengths of your dog, but also look at what he cannot do so well and see if you can find his natural opposite.

If you already have an older dog which is not used to being trained and does not seem to be interested, I have the following tips for you:

The most effective way to increase the readiness of your dog to work with you is hunger. If he is hungry enough, he will show readiness. You may think that this method is cruel but let me take away your fears. I am not talking about starving him for weeks until he is under-nourished. On the contrary, I am suggesting only to leave out one or two meals to intensify his appetite. Also, you should not try to train him directly after feeding.

And you do not need to worry about your Rhodesian Ridgeback if he does not receive his food for a limited length of time. Remember that he is descended from the wolves and it is normal for them to go without food for a few days. Even a few centuries later, it is the same for your Rhodesian Ridgeback. Some breeders even recommend feeding your dog only six times a week and generally fasting on the other day.

We humans, who are used to eating daily, find it hard to understand. You can believe me that it will not damage your relationship with your dog. Just try it and be surprised how much more his willingness to work becomes.

It is also important that you use treats during training, later they can be deducted from his meal before you find yourself with a completely different problem – overweight!

As you can see, dog training is much more than throwing a stick. You have to analyse the breed characteristics and the individual preferences of your Rhodesian Ridgeback. The most important thing: build on them and find a suitable training programme.

This may sound like a lot of responsibility for you and very complicated. However, it is considerably easier than you think. As in all things, no-one is born a master.

You will both be beginners and will grow into the challenge. Especially at the beginning, you need to find out what you both enjoy. As soon as you have found something suitable, the rest will follow. I am sure of that.

## WHAT DOES YOUR RHODESIAN RIDGEBACK NEED TO KNOW ALREADY?

As I already mentioned, this guidebook is only suitable for owners and dogs who have completed their basic training. You will not learn how to train basic commands in this book.

If you do not yet have a dog or puppy or if you have not finished the basic training yet, I recommend my book "Rhodesian Ridgeback Training – Dog Training for your Rhodesian Ridgeback puppy". That guidebook will prepare you both well for the training which is to be found in this book.

Your dog should be able to perform the following actions without hesitation:

- Sit
- Lie down
- Stay
- Recall
- Finish exercise
- Giving something up

Be absolutely honest: Is your dog able to do all these exercises?

To be sure that we are talking about the same thing: I mean that your Rhodesian Ridgeback should be able to respond to these commands wherever he is and despite any distractions and perform them correctly.

Can he do that?

I have often heard from dog owners that their dogs "nearly always come back" when they are called and that is enough for them. Honestly, that is not enough. If you have no expectations of your Rhodesian Ridgeback in everyday life and let him do, more or less, what he wants, why should he obey you when you need him to - particularly if he is playing with other dogs, or has smelled something interesting or plain cannot be bothered?

It is important that you understand the nature of your dog before you begin with dog training. Particularly with a breed like that of a Rhodesian Ridgeback, you can not see the ancestery of the wolf as easily as with a Husky, but it is there. Wolves live in packs. Despite centuries of breeding, the basic instincts of the wolfpack remains within the Rhodesian Ridgeback.

That means for you: In a pack, there is a clear structure. At the top is the pack leader. You can recognise him through his self-confidence, he takes responsibility and always knows what he wants. He ensures discipline and does not tolerate disobedience. And that not only sometimes, but always.

If your Rhodesian Ridgeback does not think you are up to the job, he will want to take over the position. Unfortunately, he will not be able to cope with it. He will not be able to estimate dangers correctly, which can bring him into dangerous situations. This includes, for example, the dangers of approaching vehicles or the long-term effects of human food on his body. However, you can. It is imperative that you assume the role of pack leader, even if it is difficult and people may make fun of you.

As pack leader you must be one hundred percent sure that your Rhodesian Ridgeback ALWAYS and RELIABLY obeys the commands previously mentioned.

If you cannot confirm that with a good conscience, I strongly suggest that you perfect the basic training before continuing with this training book. After many years of experience, you can believe me when I say it will be significantly better for you and your Rhodesian Ridgeback.

To conclude this chapter, I would like to add something which you must be able to do in order to successfully train your dog:

You must know how important it is to be consistent. There is absolutely no point in permitting and encouraging your dog to do something one day and forbidding him to do it the next. You should also follow my suggestions one-to-one because there is always a reason why I suggest that and nothing else. Consistent and exact implementation is the key to success. Failure to do so will result in not achieving the success which you are both capable of. Please always remember that.

**The most important facts for you and your Rhodesian Ridgeback at a quick glance:**

1. The breed of your dog, the Rhodesian Ridgeback, is suited to all three types of training. Try each of them and find out which is the most fun for him as an individual and not as a breed – but do not forget: you should also have fun.

2. Make sure that you do not overstress your Rhodesian Ridgeback. You should also not underestimate the danger of an addiction.

3. It is important that your Rhodesian Ridgeback blindly obeys all the basic commands. In addition, you must also ensure that you stick to the smallest of detail in the instructions in a consistent manner.

# - Chapter 4 -

# PHYSICAL TRAINING

## WHAT IS PHYSICAL TRAINING?

Physical training is the form of training which most people are familiar with. Contrary to a lack of mental stimulation, a lack of physical stimulation can be easily recognised. When a dog runs around excitedly, greets his owner raucously and possibly comes to greet his owner with his lead in his mouth, everyone can see what he wants. It is also clear that many owners are more aware of their dogs' physical needs, rather than their mental ones.

Even though people are aware and accept that physical training is necessary, it is often misunderstood. Most owners believe that they have done enough for their physical well-being to take them out once or twice a day. This may be enough for one or two breeds but particularly with Rhodesian Ridgebacks I can tell you that it is not enough.

Your Rhodesian Ridgeback has an innate desire for physical exercise and you must ensure that he gets it.

Here, as in life generally, it makes more sense to have a sensible strategy and plan than to go head first into it.

Therefore, we should agree that taking your Rhodesian Ridgeback round the block once a day for him to do his business or perhaps take a longer walk is not physical training. Let's be honest: Is your dog exhausted afterwards and does he lie down on his blanket, when he comes back, to sleep for 1 or 2 hours? If this is not the case when you come back from your daily trip then, although you have taken him out, which is necessary and proper, you have not been training with him.

Physical training means that you have got the best out of yourselves in close cooperation with each other. It is important that you and your Rhodesian Ridgeback have worked together to burn off all your extra energy in a relatively short time. It is not to be confused with the classical "walk" where the owner and his dog walk next to each other without any requirement for closely working together. With physical training, that is exactly the focus. It is not only about burning off excess energy but also the close cooperation between the two of you.

In the previous chapter I already mentioned that it is important to decide which type of training suits your Rhodesian Ridgeback. If you have got yourself an almost hyperactive companion, who seems to have an endless amount of energy, although it is important to tire him out physically, I would not put the focus on that part of the training. It is this type of dog which can develop an addiction which becomes more and more demanding. This could cause problems with joints, stress and behavioural abnormalities.

Decide whether, in that case, it would be better not to follow his obvious urge and exercise him more and more, but rather to start with intelligence training in order to give him a completely new challenge. Naturally, you should always make sure that your bundle of energy gets enough exercise but it should be no more than he actually needs.

In this chapter I will mainly concentrate on two types of physical training: retrieving and dog-dangler training. Perhaps you are asking yourself why I would give retrieving an extra chapter because everyone can throw a stick. And you are right. The question is if everyone does it correctly, and there I have my doubts. Here, you will not learn how to throw a stick correctly, I assume you can do that already. Here you will learn how to turn throwing and fetching into a proper exercise which challenges both you and your dog and encourages close cooperation.

It is the same with dog-dangler training. Here I will not show you how your dog should mindlessly chase after a stuffed animal but how to control his impulses. Both exercises appear, on the surface, to be very simple. However, if you do them correctly, they will challenge him and achieve other things too – not only in the physical training sense but also in learning cooperation.

You should also be aware that both methods, retrieval and dog-dangler training, are only a fraction of the things which you could do with your dog. However, I specifically chose these two methods because they offer the advantage of not needing to spend much money on them. In addition, neither method is as complex as, for example, agility training, which is difficult to explain in a guidebook. Bearing in mind that my aspiration for this book is that you can start on them immediately after you finish reading, I think this is the best choice.

In the last chapter I will give you some more suggestions on how you can expand on your training, using additional methods. For those methods I would recommend, however, that you visit a dog training school which offers special courses. Here, a guidebook is often not enough.

## WHAT ARE THE ADVANTAGES?

The advantages of physical training are quickly listed:

- Firstly, it serves, as the name suggests, to physically challenge your dog. The aim is to tire him out most effectively in a short period of time.
- Secondly, it is a perfect method for you to strengthen the bond with your dog. You will need to become a committed team in order that you can carry out the exercises correctly. You will notice quickly, how attentive your Rhodesian Ridgeback will become and how quickly he reacts to your instructions.
- Last, but not least, this training has the enormous advantage that it produces a large number of Endorphins (happy hormones) in the body. This will always be the case when he has successfully mastered a task, for example, when he has caught a ball and receives a treat from you. And you will also produce Endorphins when you see the reaction of your dog to your commands and

when you notice how happily he carries them out. The dog training will ensure that you both produce an abundance of hormones which will strengthen your bond.

What do you think? Are these enough advantages for you to want to start physical training?

If not, I have an additional, very important, advantage for you:

Physical training suits your Rhodesian Ridgeback's temperament perfectly. Normally, he loves exercise and is very good at learning new commands. For that, this training will be of great benefit to him. All his inbred characteristics indicate this. As most Rhodesian Ridgebacks possess a strong hunting instinct, he will love retrieving and dog-dangler training.

# INTRODUCTION OF THE TRAINING METHODS

RETRIEVAL

I have already mentioned that the Rhodesian Ridgeback is descended from the wolf. Because of this, it is natural for your Rhodesian Ridgeback to catch prey, take it into its mouth and possibly take it to another place in order to eat it. It is this propensity which is used during retrieval exercises. However, the emphasis in this case is not on killing its prey but on the fun, he will experience in the cooperation with you.

With your Rhodesian Ridgeback, you have chosen a breed with a strong hunting instinct. It will probably be easy for him to enjoy this type of training. However, there are exceptions and it is possible that you may have to awaken his enthusiasm for retrieval games.

But what exactly is retrieval? Retrieval is an exercise which substitutes the hunt for a lifeless prey. The routine is basically always the same. You throw the prey and he brings it back to you. The advantage of this is clear. You do not need any equipment other than a retrieval object.

If you have any reservations about strengthening his hunting instinct, let me say this to you:

Your Rhodesian Ridgeback, whether he has a hunting instinct or not, never "just" goes for a walk. He does not look at the nice scenery or the flowers on the side of the path. He is always consciously searching for prey or an interesting scent which is worth pursuing. This is where retrieval training starts. It is perfectly suited to using the natural instincts of your Rhodesian Ridgeback. It also has a positive effect in that it shows your Rhodesian Ridgeback that you know exactly what he enjoys and that you approve of his impulses in this case.

In addition, it also achieves the following:

- That you always hunt together
- That you, the human, decide what will be hunted next
- That you give the start command
- That you decide on the type of hunt
- That you share the prey, and
- That you decide when the hunt is finished.

In other words, through the retrieval training, you support his hunting instinct, perhaps even strengthening it. However, if you carry out this training correctly, you show your dog, at the same time, that hunting with you is much better and more fun than hunting alone.

If you become a clearly-communicating leading figure, who always knows when the next enjoyable hunt will take place, offers various strategies and provides fun and orientation, the lonely hunt will become ever more unattractive.

How best do you start retrieval training?

Firstly, you need to find the right retrieval object. Some dogs do not care at all what prey they are to fetch, but there are those which need to see a purpose in each exercise. For these dogs, and perhaps your Rhodesian Ridgeback will be one of these, it makes no sense for them to simply run after a ball which you have thrown.

For this type of dog, I recommend training with a dummy training pouch. This way your Rhodesian Ridgeback will be hunting something which it can really eat, as long as he sticks to the commands. This makes sense to even the most demanding dog. Training pouches are available in most pet shops and are not expensive.

Once you have found a suitable object you should start in small steps before you allow your Rhodesian Ridgeback to fetch. Let him carry out the commands that he already knows, such as "sit". As a reward, he will be allowed to take his treat out of the training pouch, which you will hold in front of him.

Repeat that several times, so that your dog associates the training pouch with a reward and feeding. As soon as you think he has understood the association, you can drag the dummy training pouch along the ground. When you see that he is following the pouch attentively and is watching every move you make, you can throw the training pouch onto the floor, a small distance away from you. But be careful: You must ensure that this game does not turn into a tug of war. You do not want to condition him so that he will not return the pouch.

When your Rhodesian Ridgeback runs after the training pouch you should praise him lavishly. If he does not run after it, you need to start again from the beginning because his interest was probably not strong enough or perhaps you have thrown the pouch too far.

Once your dog has the training pouch in his mouth, encourage him with your voice and body language to run to you. When your Rhodesian Ridgeback begins to run towards you, you give him the command "fetch". Your dog should then begin to associate that command with carrying the pouch.

Important: Do not use the command to entice him towards you. At the beginning it is important that he only hears this command when he is already doing it. This way the association between the action and the command is understood much more quickly.

As soon as he arrives at your feet, take the pouch off him – here you should probably use the command "drop" – and you give him a treat out of the pouch.

You can see how important it is for your dog to know the basic commands, such as the "come here" and "drop" signals. If your dog is still having problems with those commands, I recommend using a long lead. That way you can ensure that your dog focuses on the prey and not on escaping. You must ensure that your

Rhodesian Ridgeback does not manage to open the pouch without you because the main aim of this exercise is that he only gets his reward through you.

Once your dog masters this exercise at a short distance, you can slowly increase the difficulty by throwing the pouch further.

Once your dog has mastered the command "fetch", and depending on your dog's nature, you can increase the distance even further.

Below you will find a few alternatives to make this training more interesting and challenging than just throwing a training pouch.

- **Vary the surroundings:** Change the venue from the house to the garden, from the garden to the fields, from the fields to the woods. Your dog will be challenged by the different kinds of distractions he will face. His job is to ignore them while he is training. Even though it sounds simple, it will be a real challenge for him to ignore the different smells, people and animals.

- **Change the ground surface:** Let your Rhodesian Ridgeback retrieve his pouch in, for example, long grass, or if you have a waterproof pouch and a dog that loves swimming, you can throw the pouch into a stream or river.
- **Change the starting time:** Throw the pouch and have your Rhodesian Ridgeback wait in the "sit" position until you give the command which allows him to run after his prey. You cannot believe how difficult an exercise it is, physically and mentally, to wait and keep still.
- **Vary the number of pouches:** Why only throw one pouch? Combine this physical training with memory training. Make your Rhodesian Ridgeback wait in the "sit" position and throw two pouches at the same time, then give the command to "fetch". Now he has to remember where both pouches have landed. Of course, you can vary the number and train him with a command which pouch he should retrieve first.

You will notice how much more there is to retrieval than just running after a stick. When wolves hunt in packs, communication is the most important thing for them. If they do not communicate properly, they will not be successful in the hunt, which in turn can have fatal consequences. This is why wolves communicate very clearly and pay attention to every nuance.

Unfortunately, today many dogs do not understand their owners and vice versa and this can lead to misunderstandings and problems. Through the retrieval training you will learn the language of your dog and your Rhodesian Ridgeback will understand your language. A strong relationship can only develop when both parties can understand each other.

Thoughtful and consistent retrieval training will improve the attention span, concentration and fitness of your Rhodesian Ridgeback. It will also improve his obedience, his trust and his relationship with you.

However, as I mentioned at the beginning, not every dog enjoys running after objects and bringing them back to you. Some dogs do not need added difficulties but are happy to do the same things over and over again.

Both of these things are perfectly normal. It is important that you read these signs correctly and do not try to push your dog to do something which he does not want to.

If you are not sure how to do the training properly, there are a number of retrieval courses at dog schools which I can wholeheartedly recommend to you.

**Why retrieval exercises are a useful training for you and your Rhodesian Ridgeback at a quick glance:**

1. Retrieval training is a perfect match for the Rhodesian Ridgeback breed.
2. It satisfies the natural instinct of your Rhodesian Ridgeback and helps him to find an interesting alternative to hunting on his own.
3. Running backwards and forwards not only keeps him fit but waiting for the start commands and noticing various objects will also be mentally demanding on your Rhodesian Ridgeback, something which is very important with this breed.
4. You have found a training method which you can use anywhere, whether at home, in the garden or while travelling. You only need your pouch and off you go.

## DOG-DANGLER TRAINING

Training with danglers and retrieval training are both activities which trigger the hunting instinct of your Rhodesian Ridgeback. Naturally, it is possible that you amplify his hunting instinct or even awake it with this type of training.

However, this is not the aim of this exercise. Originally, the dog-dangler was used for training the hunt. The idea was not only to simulate hunting a fleeing animal but was also used to control his basic instincts.

What does this mean, exactly?

Dog-dangler training is aimed at giving an alternative to the hunt and to tire him out but also to teach him obedience under difficult conditions and take control of his impulses. It helps no-one if your Rhodesian Ridgeback runs out of control, chasing a wild animal or cat. It could even be life-threatening for your dog, for he may not notice approaching cars or other dangers.

This is the purpose of the dog-dangler training. The dog-dangler is an extension of your arm which allows you to imitate interesting hunting games while at the same time being able to control the behaviour of your

Rhodesian Ridgeback under safe conditions, perhaps also with the use of a long lead. It is a completely different challenge than simply running after fleeing wild animals on the side of the road.

When you train your Rhodesian Ridgeback with the dog-dangler, he will learn to obey your commands, despite having the additional distraction of his hunt. This means he will be able to break off his hunt and sit quietly at your command. He will also learn that he cannot start his hunt until you give the command. This also applies to playing with other dogs. The correct training will mean that he will be capable of remaining attentive to your wishes and will wait for your command before running off.

Does this sound as if it could be the right kind of training for you and your Rhodesian Ridgeback? Do you think you could both benefit from such training? If so, you will discover below how it works.

It is important that you only start this training with an adult dog. The physical exertion is intense for short periods of time and not suitable for the growth of a puppy's joints. Your Rhodesian Ridgeback also needs to be fully healthy. Of course, your dog should also have a certain amount of predatory instinct for this training to be useful. If he does not have that and does not even enjoy training when hungry, this is not the right training for him.

What do you need for this training?

Normally, you do not need much. You should possess a dog-dangler which is made from a rod and a cord. You can purchase one or make it yourself. The basic principle is: the bigger the dog, the bigger the dog-dangler should be. I recommend a rod length of about 2 metres for a fully-grown Rhodesian Ridgeback and a cord of approximately the same length. You can, of course, use a huge rod but it should be flexible, light and pliable. That makes the training much simpler.

The important thing about the cord is that it should not be too fine. You should never use a fishing line because this could cause serious injury to your dog's mouth when he snaps at it. I recommend a thickness of at least 4 millimetres.

It depends on your Rhodesian Ridgeback what you use as "prey". What does he particularly like? You can attach a toy, a food-pouch or just a piece of fabric. It does not matter as long as your Rhodesian Ridgeback is interested enough in it. Similar to retrieval, some dogs need to see a purpose behind what they are doing, which they would, for example, when they are chasing a food-pouch.

I mentioned at the beginning of this book that your dog needs to have completed his basic training so that he can carry out the basic commands without fail. This also applies to dog-dangler training. He must know the commands "sit", "lie down" and "stay". For this exercise he also needs to know "sit" at a distance. If this is not the case, I recommend strongly that you teach him this first, because otherwise the dog-dangler training will not be useful.

Once your dog has mastered the above commands, you can begin to interest him for his "prey". Start by putting the prey on the dog-dangler, close to your Rhodesian Ridgeback and swinging it in swift moves across the ground.

My tip: Practise the movements first without your Rhodesian Ridgeback because it is not as easy as you may think. You need some practice at moving the dog-dangler in quick, smooth movements, particularly when your dog reacts quickly to the stimulus and runs energetically towards it. So practice a little bit before you start training with him.

If your Rhodesian Ridgeback shows interest in the game and runs after the prey, you should reward him by giving him a short chasing game. Do not let him catch the prey. Instead, after the short hunt, lift the pouch up above the ground and bring it towards you. Give the command "sit" and wait until your Rhodesian Ridgeback obeys. As a reward you can let the prey go, giving the "end of exercise" sign (I use "go on" but you can use any other word you choose) and let him chase it again.

You can repeat this exercise until your Rhodesian Ridgeback obeys the "sit" command without hesitation once you have the prey in your hand.

Because this training is tiring for your Rhodesian Ridgeback, you should restrict it to about 15 minutes. At the beginning it should be a lot shorter than that. Take care of your dog and his ligaments and joints. Dog-dangler training is high-performance sport. In addition, I would recommend a short warm-up period before you begin training. Take a gentle stroll of about

15-20 minutes with him. It will warm his muscles and reduce the danger of injury, just as with us humans.

After your Rhodesian Ridgeback has mastered the basics of the dog-dangler training, it is time to learn more difficult exercises:

- **Do not just rush into it:** Your Rhodesian Ridgeback must learn that he must not just run off and chase after the prey. He must always wait for the signal word "go on" before he runs. You can train him to do that by varying the above exercise. Tell your Rhodesian Ridgeback to "sit". Only when he is sitting, relaxed, should you throw the prey onto the ground, a short distance from him. When he wants to stand up, you give him the command "stay". If he remains seated, wait a few seconds before giving him the "go on" command, allowing him to chase the prey again. Extend the time between the two commands as time goes on.

  If your Rhodesian Ridgeback does not stay when you give the command, take the prey away quickly by pulling it off the ground and taking it into your hand. Make him sit and try again. Once he is able to carry out your wishes, over a longer time-period, you can start to increase the amount of stimulus you give him. Move the prey faster towards him and away from him. Zigzag around him and move it abruptly. Your Rhodesian Ridgeback should sit all the time you are carrying out these manoeuvres. If he stands up, take the prey away and start again from the beginning. Your Rhodesian Ridgeback should only be allowed to satisfy his hunting instinct if he has correctly carried out your commands.

- **"Sit" during the hunt.** The next step in difficulty is to command your dog to stop the hunt and sit down without taking the prey out of the hunt. The basic requirement for this is that he is proficient in the "stop at a distance" command. I also recommend that you do not start with that exercise until your dog is very tired and has already hunted his prey a few times. It is also useful for another person to use the dog-dangler so that you can concentrate fully on your Rhodesian Ridgeback.

This is how you start the exercise: After you have tired your dog out with the hunt exercises, wave the prey in a slower and more leisurely manner. Give him the start command "go on". As soon as he has started the hunt, give him the command "sit" without taking the prey out of the game. If he does not sit immediately, lift the prey up and take it into your hand. Give the command "sit" once again and start the exercise from the beginning.

With some dogs it will be necessary at the beginning to stand in front of your dog to make him sit.

The moment he sits correctly, even if for a fraction of a second, you can give him the signal "go on" and allow him to chase the prey once again. The prey should be moving all the time and not stand still.

If you are successful with that, you can increase the difficulty again. Please take small steps with this exercise. It is very demanding and will challenge your dog to the maximum. It is not easy for him to stop an exercise in the middle and sit down, so please do not despair if your Rhodesian Ridgeback fails many times and you have to break up the hunt and start again. Perhaps you could go back to practising the exercise "sit at a distance".

Once your Rhodesian Ridgeback has mastered this exercise, you will be able to get your dog to sit, even by the highest stimulus and maximum distraction of a quickly moving prey or in the company of a playmate, and he should not continue the hunt without your permission.

- **"Lie down" during the hunt:** This exercise is an extension to the previous one. Instead of giving the command "sit", you give your Rhodesian Ridgeback the command "lie down". You should only start with this training when the previous "sit" command is no problem to your Rhodesian Ridgeback, otherwise it will be counter-productive. You also need a lot of patience for this exercise until your dog has mastered it. You will reach your goal through repetition and consistency.

- **Giving up the prey:** There are a lot of trainers who say that a Rhodesian Ridgeback should never be able to touch its prey. My opinion: It is not possible to avoid that. No matter how well you can manipulate the dog-dangler, at some point your dog will grab it. The important thing if this happens is that you react correctly. Here you should react as if you were doing retrieval training and allow your dog to bring the prey to you. It is very important that this happens faultlessly and your Rhodesian Ridgeback always gives back the prey voluntarily. As a reward, he is given a treat out of the pouch.

If you follow these training tips you will be surprised how your relationship with your dog will develop. Remember, the aim of the exercise is not only to tire out your dog but also to be able to control his impulses. This is only possible if he concentrates both on the prey AND you. He must be able to block out everything else.

With this exercise you also give your dog a chance to satisfy his natural hunting instinct and at the same time build a basis so that uncontrolled hunting can be avoided.

The best thing about it is: You do not need to use an expensive dog school or expensive materials, nor need you go to instruction classes yourself. As ever with dog training, it is about consistency, timing and repetition. Any dog owner who remembers these three main points, can successfully carry out dog-dangler training.

**Why dog-dangler training is so useful for you and your Rhodesian Ridgeback – at a glance:**

1. Dog-dangler training is perfect for the inbred characteristics of your Rhodesian Ridgeback.
2. Your Rhodesian Ridgeback not only receives an exciting alternative to hunting on his own, but also stays in contact with you during the hunt – this represents an achievement which can not be bought for money.
3. The training is extremely effective. 15 minutes are enough to tire out your bundle of energy.
4. Rhodesian Ridgebacks have been bred to react to commands as well as to act independently. It is these two characteristics which are put to the test with this exercise. Your Rhodesian Ridgeback can develop his own strategies to obtain his prey but is at the same time able to obey you and your commands.

## MORE SUGGESTIONS

With the retrieval and dog-dangler training you have now learned two possibilities to train your Rhodesian Ridgeback physically and to improve your relationship with him. As mentioned previously, these are not the only two forms of training.

Below I will introduce three more types of training, which I find very useful. They are more complex and, in my opinion, need the help of a professional trainer, so I will not go into great detail here. If you are interested in these, I suggest going to a good dog school near you which specialises in them.

Now we come to the first of the three training methods:

**Agility training:** Agility training originates in England and is very similar to show jumping in equine sport. This is similar to these show jumping tournaments. The aim is agility and that your Rhodesian Ridgeback learns to negotiate an obstacle course. Examples of such obstacles are seesaws, catwalks, tunnels, tyres or slaloms. This type of training not only improves your Rhodesian Ridgeback's control and skill, but also improves cooperation between you. At first you learn to master the obstacles together, and later you determine the sequence.

Recently, agility training has become something of a fashionable sport which most dog-owners have heard of. The only reservation I have with this is the danger of obsession by your Rhodesian Ridgeback. Speak about this with your trainer if your Rhodesian Ridgeback already possess an extremely high readiness for intense physical exercise. Apart from that, agility training can be recommended without fear of harm.

The second type of training that I would like to show you is **Treibball**.

This is meant particularly for sheepdogs but there are individual breeds which can have a lot of fun with this exercise. Naturally, this training does not represent one-for-one a flock of sheep but it is very close.

With Treibball training your dog will manoeuvre gymnastic balls into a goal. This may seem easy but in fact it is very complex. Your Rhodesian Ridgeback must work independently and focused, only guided by verbal commands from you. This means that you must make yourself understood at a distance and your

Rhodesian Ridgeback must be able to learn quickly, stay concentrated and obey you at all times.

The difficulty of the exercise can be increased by increasing the number of balls or defining new routes. As this training is very complex, you should not attempt this without the help of a professional trainer. Books and videos are not enough in this instance. Even the correct choice of ball and the first contact of the dog with it can result in many mistakes being made, which will affect the training at a later stage.

The third type of training is also similar to horse training. It is called **lunging**. It may seem strange to hear at first but a dog can be lunged in a successful and effective way. This type of sport is relatively new but has a great potential, proven by the fact that is becoming increasingly popular.

Like horse-lunging, the dog will run along a lunging circle, which is normally marked out in advance. The dog must follow your commands and carry out particular exercises, sometimes with obstacles. You as the command-giver would stand inside the circle at all times and guide your Rhodesian Ridgeback from a distance.

Classical commands, which are to be followed, are, for example, "go on", "stay", running to the left or the right. At the beginning, a lead is usually used to enable better control. However, the aim is for your dog to obey the commands without a lead.

As with the other methods, I would recommend getting help from a professional trainer. This training is also too complex to be able to learn at home.

I hope I could give you a few ideas in this chapter as to what kind of extra training you can do with your dog.

If you want to use a training method which is suitable for a Rhodesian Ridgeback but you are not a hunter yourself, even though there are a lot of alternatives, I recommend hunt-orientated training, such as retrieval or dog-dangler.

# - Chapter 5 -

# INTELLIGENCE TRAINING

## WHAT IS INTELLIGENCE TRAINING?

Contrary to physical training, intelligence is the lesser-known training method. Because it is so little-known, perhaps you are asking yourself why there is such a thing as intelligence training for dogs?

Very simple:

Dogs are rational creatures and can be very intelligent. Depending on the breed, some dogs are born with a certain amount of intelligence, but there are some breeds where this is more or less pronounced.

With your Rhodesian Ridgeback you have not chosen a dog of the most intelligent breed, but he is still able to understand things quickly. He can learn new commands, after 25 to 40 repeats, which is about average. I can only recommend encouraging this intelligence because every rational creature wants to utilise its knowledge and intelligence to its best advantage. Similar to training muscles, your Rhodesian Ridgeback will want to use his brain after he has learned something. Pure physical training will not be enough for a dog such as a Rhodesian Ridgeback if you want to give him an environment appropriate to his breed.

It is the same with people: If we are underchallenged, it affects our moods and our bad moods affect our behaviour. Your Rhodesian Ridgeback will suffer in the same way, so it is important that you occupy him mentally as well as physically.

How do you do that?

There are two ways to do this. One way is with targeted training. With that I mean that your Rhodesian Ridgeback will learn the commands "sit" and "lie down" or must sit in front of his food bowl and wait until he is given the command to start eating.

These are exercises which require clear behavioural patterns. The main aim of the training is to recognise these patterns and then to repeat them constantly. Your dog will be rewarded immediately when he demonstrates the correct behaviour which, in turn, encourages him to keep doing it.

You have already successfully established this type of behaviour in some areas of his training. Also, the special chapter with the title "Fun Training" deals with this. It is an excellent way to stimulate your Rhodesian Ridgeback mentally, but it is not the only way.

I would like to show you a different type of training in this chapter. With this, the aim is not to train your Rhodesian Ridgeback to achieve a certain goal, but to give him tasks where he has to find his own solution.

Finding solutions to problems stimulates his brain in a particular way, especially with dogs which were once hounds, like your Rhodesian Ridgeback, which had been bred for such purposes over hundreds of years.

For this reason, I am suggesting the following training methods in this chapter: Searching for food, scent training and memory training.

You will discover the advantages of these training methods in the following pages.

## WHAT ARE THE ADVANTAGES?

There are many advantages in intelligence training, which does not only concentrate on recognising and repeating behavioural patterns, but on solving problems.

Firstly, it enables you to find out the true nature of your Rhodesian Ridgeback. Contrary to physical training and recognising and repeating behavioural patterns, he will be able to utilise his own ideas for the first time.

You will quickly see whether your Rhodesian Ridgeback is creative and inventive and if he is a team-player or prefers to find his own solutions. And most importantly, you will see how closely he can work with you.

In order to achieve this, you must ensure that you always set the tasks so that your Rhodesian Ridgeback does not solve the them using behavioural recognition. The tasks should always test his skill, his use of strategies or his cooperation with you – his human pack leader.

Another advantage is that this training not only challenges the intelligence and creativity of your Rhodesian Ridgeback but also yours. You will also be challenged to find exciting and varied training tasks for you both.

I am not worried about that; you do not have to be a genius to do that. As with everything, this training demands consistency, timing and repetition. The most important thing here again is your enthusiasm. If you are enthusiastic and are having fun, this is transmitted to your Rhodesian Ridgeback, who will also take part in the training with delight.

Last, but not least, this training is very intensive and therefore exhausting for your Rhodesian Ridgeback. You will notice that a quarter of an hour "nose work" (for example searching for food) will tire your Rhodesian Ridgeback out much quicker than active physical exercise.

If he is enthusiastically working on his task, he will be only too happy to rest afterwards and sleep a while. This effect is particularly noticeable in sporting "aces" who are normally not easy to tire out.

What do you think? Does it sound like a good exercise for you and your Rhodesian Ridgeback?

## IS YOUR DOG INTELLIGENT?

Perhaps you are asking yourself if your Rhodesian Ridgeback is intelligent enough for this training.

The answer is: YES!

No dog is too stupid for intelligence training. It could be that one dog learns quicker than another, but everyone can learn it, as long as the owner is patient enough and builds up the exercise step by step. Every exercise has a lot of small steps so that there are enough alternatives for the quickest and also the not-so-quick mind.

Apart from that, I always find it difficult to label anyone as clever or stupid. Like humans, one is perhaps an absolute Genius in mathematics, but has no idea how to communicate on a human level. It is similar with dogs.

For this reason, the American psychologist and dog researcher, Dr. Stanley Coren, identified three types of intelligence in dogs:

1. Instinctive intelligence: This includes everything which your Rhodesian Ridgeback inherited from its ancestors. This includes the intelligence of your Rhodesian Ridgeback, which I can confirm because of his breed.
2. Adaptive intelligence: This is the knowledge which your Rhodesian Ridgeback has obtained during life, so everything that you have taught him (or which he learned himself).
3. Work and obedience intelligence: This means how quickly your Rhodesian Ridgeback learns new commands or how often you need to repeat an exercise before he has learned it.

As with people, your Rhodesian Ridgeback could be extremely good in one thing and not in another. That is completely normal.

I personally recommend that beginners might consider to start with a breed with a rather low work and obedience intelligence. Why? Because the more intelligent the dog is, the higher are his expectations on your training and your consitency in his upbringing. As I already mentioned, he does not only learn positive things quickly, but also everything you do not want him to learn. A dog which does not learn so quickly is happier with less and is less creative in the ways in which he can avoid your commands.

Often, a dog is unjustly regarded as being stupid. His behaviour could have been caused by bad timing with the rewards, causing him not to behave as you wish him to. It could also have been caused by the fact that a particularly clever dog does not see the point of running after a ball and therefore does not want to do it, no matter how well you built up the training. In this case, the dog is not stupid but especially intelligent.

As you can see, it is not important how intelligent your Rhodesian Ridgeback is but how well you deal with his level of intelligence.

Rhodesian Ridgebacks generally show an average intelligence as far as work and obedience are concerned. This means for you that they do not understand new commands and exercises after the first five repeats, but they also do not need a very long time to understand what you want from them. On average they need 25 to 40 repeats before they have really undertstood a new command.

You will need a little more patience with your Rhodesian Ridgeback as with, for example, a Border Collie who, according to Dr. Coren, shows the greatest work and obedience intelligence. However, your little rascal is a lot less demanding and is more tolerant towards small lacks in finesse during training, which is worth its weight in gold for beginners.

Nevertheless, you should try to carry out the exercises with your Rhodesian Ridgeback as cleanly and accurately as you can. There is a reason why they are built-up as they are.

## INTRODUCTION OF THE TRAINING METHODS

### FORAGING FOR FOOD

Foraging for food is the first intelligence training method I would like to introduce to you. As you have probably guessed, it involves your Rhodesian Ridgeback finding his own food. In most cases, he will fall back on his sense of smell, something we call "nose work" in dog training.

Why is nose work so exciting for dogs?

Humans have about 5 million olfactory (smell) cells in our noses, whereas most dog breeds have 200 million of them. This means that they understand their environment very differently to us.

Your Rhodesian Ridgeback belongs to the front-runners when it comes to olfactory cells, having more than 225 million, only beaten by the sniffing king, the Bloodhound, who has 75 million more than him.

Did you know that your Rhodesian Ridgeback, in contrast to humans, is not only capable of picking up which different scents he is smelling, and with which intensity each, but also with which nostril he is smelling them. This means he can determine from which direction each scent is coming from and where the prey is going. In addition, your Rhodesian Ridgeback can identify individual scents and sort them. It is these characteristics which predestines him for the food forage exercise.

Searching for food has another advantage. The search stems from the natural lifestyle of your dog and imitates his innate instincts: Searching for tracks, catching prey, eating. There is hardly an exercise which can top that. This exercise also calls for team play. Your Rhodesian Ridgeback will learn that you have almost the same capabilities as him and that the exercise is worth giving it his attention and following your commands. After all, you always know where there are tracks, prey and food for him.

It is important to build up the exercises correctly and to pay attention to certain things from the outset:

- You should always keep him on the lead, if you are not training in your own garden, so that you are in control of your Rhodesian Ridgeback at all times.

- Particularly at the beginning, you should ensure that the training area does not have many distractions. I prefer to train in my home at the start, then the garden. I only go out into the woods and fields when I am sure that the exercise has been mastered. You should make sure that there are no other animals close by because you are working with food, which could also be interesting for passing creatures.
- Ensure that your Rhodesian Ridgeback only searches after you have given the command. It is very important that he learns from the beginning that you are the person giving the commands because otherwise he will be constantly looking for food and could eat anything he finds.
- Learn the body language of your Rhodesian Ridgeback and ensure that he does not overdo it.

Now that you know what to watch out for, we can start building up the exercise. As always, we start with a simple, basic exercise in finding food and it goes as follows:

Stand next to your Rhodesian Ridgeback and let a small treat fall on the floor in front of him. Draw his attention to it by using an encouraging voice and hand signals. As soon as your Rhodesian Ridgeback shows interest and moves towards the treat, give him the command "find it". As soon as he has eaten the treat, let the next treat fall and keep repeating the exercise.

Once your dog has internalised the exercise, you can start walking forward during the exercise and drop a treat every now and again. When the exercise is successful and you have no problems with it, drop a treat when your dog is not looking towards you. Repeat this variation a few times. The aim of the exercise is for your Rhodesian Ridgeback to link the command "find it" with the search, finding and eating of the treat.

Once you are sure that your dog has made the link, you can go on to step 2. Please be absolutely sure that he understands the command, because it makes no sense to start too early with step 2. That would only over-strain your four-legged friend and you do not want that, do you?

When he understands what he has to do, you can go to the next grade of difficulty by integrating the commands "sit", "lie down" and "stay". This is how you can teach that:

Give your Rhodesian Ridgeback the command "sit" and immediately the command "stay". As soon as he is sitting, relaxed, walk a few paces away from him, show him the treat and allow it to fall a short distance from you. Now wait, at first for just a few seconds, before giving him the start signal "find it". As soon as he has found the treat, and eaten it, praise him and repeat the exercise. In time, you can increase the distance and the waiting time but be careful to increase the difficulty slowly, so that he does not overstrain himself.

The next step is to allow the food to fall in a less obvious place, to hide it slightly. Cracks, holes, piles of leaves or small containers are good places to hide the treats. Be creative and use your imagination. At first your dog can watch you, while you hide the treats, but slowly you should make it more difficult by secretly hiding the treats.

You can see that searching for food can be much fun for both of you and you can have a lot of adventures together. But what can you do if your Rhodesian Ridgeback is not interested in searching for food? It could be that your dog is not hungry so that the search does not present a stimulus for him. If this is the case, I would recommend leaving out one meal or perhaps feeding him exclusively from the search game. Do not be afraid to do that, it is not cruelty, in fact it is appropriate for his species, as wild dogs always have to hunt for their food before they can eat.

It could be, that he has not linked the words "find it" with food. If this is the case, please start again with the basic exercise and work intensively with him over a longer period of time.

If your Rhodesian Ridgeback starts to search but is unable to find his treat, there are probably too many distractions in your training area. Change the place of training and start again from the beginning. As I previously mentioned, I start every training within my own four walls. Moreover, you might choose a treat with a strong smell, which makes it much easier for your Rhodesian Ridgeback.

If your Rhodesian Ridgeback does not wait for the command "find it" but runs straight towards his treat, you must keep him on a shorter lead. Do not give him the possibility of reaching his treat before you are able to give the command. Only give him the command and extend the length of his lead when he is sitting, relaxed – and, at some point, he will do that. The winner is the one of you who has the most patience.

Should your Rhodesian Ridgeback bark non-stop, bite on the lead or show another form of impatience and protest, it could be a sign that he is not prepared to trust you or that he does not understand your signals. If this happens, I recommend finding professional help. This is also beneficial if any other problems occur which can not be solved using my tips. In cases like this, it is always advisable to have your behaviour watched and analysed.

If the exercise with treats as a search object does not suit you, you can substitute the treats for your dog's favourite toy. However, this form of searching does not always suit your dog.

You can increase the difficulty of this exercise by hiding the food in more difficult places to find. Be creative and keep thinking of new hiding places. You could try hiding the treats in tins or boxes. But please remember with this exercise: Not every dog likes the most difficult variation. It is quite acceptable if your Rhodesian Ridgeback is happy with simpler exercises.

**The reasons why searching for food is good training for you and your dog - at a glance:**

1. Like all other breeds, Rhodesian Ridgebacks love to sniff around – however there are few breeds which are adapted so well as the Rhodesian Ridgeback.
2. Rhodesian Ridgebacks are working dogs and therefore are quite happy to work for their food.
3. Cooperation within the pack is particularly important with hounds. They also cooperate in the search for food. Especially, if you start with an advanced form of the food search where the search is much more difficult, perhaps so difficult, that your dog cannot reach it without your help. Because like other dogs, Rhodesian Ridgebacks tend to become disrespectful and to see themselves as the pack leader when treated inattentively.
4. The food search satisfies a basic instinct for your Rhodesian Ridgeback. It is important that he knows that you understand and approve of it. In addition, he learns to search for food only on your command, which could even save his life.

## SCENT TRAINING

Scent training is structured much the same way as the food search. However, here the aim is not that your dog finds food but follows a specific scent. You can decide for yourself what you want to use as a scent. I recommend at the beginning using tea bags. These have the advantage that they send out a strong scent and there are many variations of them. In addition, they are small, cheap and can be found almost anywhere. If it should rain, you can put them in a plastic bag, so that they do not get wet and the scent is still strong enough for your Rhodesian Ridgeback.

As with all the exercises up to now, we will start by awaking the interest of your Rhodesian Ridgeback in the activity. Take the tea bag in your hand and look at it in a very interested and excited way. As soon as your Rhodesian Ridgeback starts to pay attention, hold the tea bag close to him. When he sniffs at it, praise him lavishly, then repeat the exercise.

Once you have the feeling that your Rhodesian Ridgeback has understood that there is a reward for him every time he sniffs at the tea bag, you can increase the difficulty.

As with the food search, you can now integrate the commands "sit" and "stay" into the exercise. When your Rhodesian Ridgeback is sitting, relaxed, go a step further and lay the tea bag theatrically on the floor. Your Rhodesian Ridgeback should stay in the sitting position while you go back to him and, with an inviting gesture, give him the "find it" command. Once he sniffs at the tea bag again, give him a huge reward. If he does not run straight towards it, you can help him by showing him the exact position of the tea bag. Repeat this exercise until your Rhodesian Ridgeback runs straight to the tea bag without delay and sniffs at it.

The next progression is to increase the distance, or you can put down the tea bag in a more hidden position. Make sure that your Rhodesian Ridgeback is always watching you. When he has understood this exercise, the next progression is pointing.

This is how you do it:

As soon as your Rhodesian Ridgeback sniffs at his tea bag, when he has found it, give him the command "sit" and only then should you give him his praise reward. Repeat that several times. Once you believe that he has understood what you are doing, by the next time you can wait a few seconds before you give the "sit" command. The aim is that he will automatically sit and wait for you. When he does this, praise him enthusiastically. If he does not do it, repeat the process a few more times before trying it again.

If he can do this too, you can start putting the tea bag in a place out of sight for your Rhodesian Ridgeback. You can, for example, go into another room in your house and put the tea bag on a stool. Return to your Rhodesian Ridgeback and give him the "find it" command. Make sure that the hiding places are not too difficult at the beginning and increase the difficulty as time goes on.

If you and your Rhodesian Ridgeback have still not had enough scent training, there is one more progression for you: You can teach him to find a particular sort of tea and to ignore the others. In order to do that, you need to start the simple way, once again.

Let your Rhodesian Ridgeback sit next to you. Lay a tea bag in full view on the floor. Go back to him and let him sniff at a tea bag of the same sort as the one you have laid out. Almost at the same time, give him the command "find it". This part is particularly important because you need to allow him to sniff at a specific sort of tea bag before you give him the command. Next, you will go through all the previous steps with the difference that you allow him to sniff at the tea bag first. You do not always have to use the same sort of tea bag. The only important thing to remember, is that the tea bag you allow him to sniff is the same sort as the one that you have laid out.

The aim is to help your Rhodesian Ridgeback understand that it is not about finding any kind of tea bag but the particular one that you have shown him. If you believe he has made that connection, you can put out two tea bags. One of them should be a different type to the one you let him sniff on. If you are successful, he will ignore the second one you have laid down and only show you the one you asked him to.

If he runs to the wrong tea bag, ignore this and give him the "find it" command once again.

Later you can use several sorts of tea and perhaps integrate food as a distraction. Make sure that you ignore it when he goes to the wrong object and only praise him when he arrives at the correct object.

As you can see, scent training is not only versatile but also offers many variations so that you two will never get bored. Apart from that, it is possible to integrate this training into everyday life as you do not need much preparation and you can do it anywhere as long as you have a tea bag with you.

My closing tip: Integrate the scent training into your daily walk. This way your Rhodesian Ridgeback's walk will turn into a small adventure. Take care that you only start doing these things when you have reached the advanced stages of the training. At the beginning, there are far too many distractions. You must be sure that your Rhodesian Ridgeback concentrates fully on the tea bag.

The great advantage of this training as opposed to the food search is that tea bags are not interesting for other animals. When you lay out food, you have to take care that it is not eaten by another dog or a wild animal. Personally, I always take a tea bag with me on a walk, together with some treats and poo bags.

## The reasons why scent training is good training for you and your dog - at a glance

1. Just like the food search, this training enables your Rhodesian Ridgeback to use his millions of olfactory (smelling) cells and indulge his sniffing instincts.
2. Contrary to the food search, you do not have to lay out food in this training, which could be interesting for other animals.
3. Your Rhodesian Ridgeback will learn to concentrate on a specific scent and ignore others, which will place a lot of demands on him.
4. You have the possibility to introduce new scents in this training, such as coins. The training can have an added advantage if your Rhodesian Ridgeback sometimes finds lost money.

## MEMORY TRAINING

Dogs are more intelligent than many people believe. What many people underestimate: Dogs have extremely good memories! It is possible to train and improve this memory the same way as it is with humans.

For this reason, I have added this training method to my book. You will probably be surprised what your dog can memorise in the shortest of time.

Contrary to the previous intelligence training, memory training is a quiet exercise. It is therefore suitable for older or sick dogs which cannot move around so easily.

Ensure that your Rhodesian Ridgeback is not too full of energy before these exercises. I recommend doing them after a walk. There is not much in the way of material. You only need a few beakers (preferably made of plastic, so that they do not break so quickly) and of course treats.

This is how you build up your exercise:

Give your Rhodesian Ridgeback the command "sit". As soon as he sits, relaxed, in front of you, show him how you put a treat into a beaker on the floor, which is placed directly in front of him. Watch how he reacts. Most dogs will put their noses or a paw on the beaker.

Wait until your Rhodesian Ridgeback knocks over the beaker and then praise him enthusiastically. Naturally, he is allowed to eat the treat as a reward. Keep repeating this exercise. Your Rhodesian Ridgeback will learn that there is a treat under the beaker and that he can get at it when he knocks the beaker over. Combine the knocking over with a command like "find the beaker". Once he has made this connection, let him wait a few seconds, before he is allowed to get at the treat. He has to learn, that this is only the case, when you give the command.

Once he has mastered this step, put out two more beakers. Hide a treat under one of the three beakers but so that he can see it. Your dog should sit close to the beakers. Make him wait a few seconds then give the command "find the beaker". Wait until he turns over the correct beaker. If he chooses the wrong beaker, stop the exercise and start again.

Only praise him when he chooses the correct beaker at the first try. When you have mastered this step, you can go on to the next one. Place another treat under one of the beakers then swap around the positions of the beakers. Let your Rhodesian Ridgeback watch what you are doing. Give him the command and praise him only when he finds the correct beaker at the first try. You can also extend the waiting time slowly to make the exercise a little more difficult.

If he is able to do this and really shows interest and enjoyment in this exercise, you can add small distractions during the waiting time. For example, make him give you his paw (you can learn how to train this in the special chapter "Fun Training") and after that he can search for the correct beaker. This way your Rhodesian Ridgeback will learn to memorize under which beaker his treat is to be found, despite distractions. The more successfully he can do this exercise, the bigger you can make the distraction.

**The reasons why memory training is good for you and your Rhodesian Ridgeback – at a glance:**

1. Memory training is different from the other two types of intelligence training. This exercise does not rely completely on your dog's sense of smell but trains the memory of your Rhodesian Ridgeback.
2. The memory training is very effective without needing a lot of equipment.
3. The better the memory training works, the easier it is to integrate other exercises, such as retrieval, when your Rhodesian Ridgeback has to remember which ball you threw where.

## OTHER IDEAS

With the forage, scent training and memory training, you have learned three methods with which you can tire your Rhodesian Ridgeback out and offer him a more interesting and challenging life.

Of course, these three methods are not the only ones. There is no limit to the creative possibilities, particularly when it comes to intelligence training. There are whole shelves of so-called intelligence games in many pet shops. I have tried some of them myself and still have a lot of fun with them. However, you do not always have to spend money on them.

You can find much cheaper alternatives to those games with everyday objects. For example, you can let your Rhodesian Ridgeback unpack his food before he eats it. You can put his food in a cardboard box wrapped in newspaper and pack that in another box. You can make it even more intensive by hiding the food from your Rhodesian Ridgeback and allowing him to look for it.

If he is successful in finding it, he still has to work to get at the food, which will present new challenges for him. Most dogs love such games which encourage them to have fun and improve their endurance.

This is a variation to his food search training, although it makes a lot of mess, as neither the cardboard box nor the newspaper will survive in one piece. I am sure that your dog will have ripped them into small pieces. If this could cause a problem for you, it is better not to try this exercise.

A further alternative to the scent or food search is detective training. Instead of him having to find his food, make him sniff out other items, such as his favourite toy. The training is built up similarly to the other two types of training. You begin with very small distances and in full view of your Rhodesian Ridgeback. It is important that you link the search command to the name of the item that he is to search for, so that he automatically links the name with the item. For example, you say, "find the ball" or "find the tiger".

This detail is important if you want to teach your Rhodesian Ridgeback to search for several items. You could, for example hide his ball and his cuddly tiger and clearly state which of the items he should search for first.

I recommend that your dog be proficient in the other trainings before you start this one, because it is a lot more challenging. The previous exercises have the advantage that the scent emanating from the tea bags is a lot stronger than that of a cuddly toy and therefore easier to master.

Let your imagination run free when deciding how to tire out your Rhodesian Ridgeback, mentally. The only thing you need to beware of is that you do not overstrain him. Build up the exercises slowly and do not expect too much too quickly. The most important thing here is repetition.

# - Chapter 6 -

# SPECIAL CHAPTER: FUN TRAINING

## WHAT IS FUN TRAINING?

After physical and intelligence training, we now arrive at my secret favourite – fun training. As I previously described, fun training is actually a sub-category of intelligence training because it deals with recognising specific behavioural patterns of your Rhodesian Ridgeback and much repetition.

Contrary to the other training methods in this book, fun training does not represent the typical behavioural patterns of your Rhodesian Ridgeback. Rather, it often reflects behavioural patterns which are not found in an animal living in the wild. The prominent feature of this training is to entertain him and to have fun.

I can understand the criticism that this training is not appropriate to the species. However, I believe that, as long as this training is additional to the other breed-appropriate training, there is nothing to say against it.

We do not want to create a circus dog, but I am sure that a few fun tricks, that you can show to your relatives, will not harm your dog. You have also learned many alternatives in this book which will satisfy the instincts of your Rhodesian Ridgeback.

## WHAT ARE THE ADVANTAGES?

Apart from the above, fun training offers several advantages for your Rhodesian Ridgeback.

- Because it belongs to intelligence training group, it clearly increases your four-legged friend's ability to concentrate.
- In addition, fun training intensifies your relationship with your Rhodesian Ridgeback. With these exercises, a great deal of cooperation is necessary from both of you.
- Last, but not least, it is a lot of fun to leave all the useful and serious training you are doing with your dog and just have a bit of fun.

Fun training is one of the few types of training that can be carried out by children. I would never expect a child to correctly follow the complex steps of dog-dangler training. But with fun training, the little ones can celebrate their first successes and at the same time learn how to train a dog properly.

For those reasons, I will share my 8 most favourite fun commands with you on the following pages. Have fun!

# INTRODUCING THE TRAINING METHODS

GIVING PAW

"Paw" is the best-known command in fun training and is seen by many as standard repertoire. You will learn here how to train that effectively.

- Give your Rhodesian Ridgeback the command "sit".
- When he is sitting, relaxed, kneel in front of him. Hold a treat in one hand. Make a fist with the other hand and hold it slightly to the side of your dog. He will move his weight automatically to one side because you are not holding your hand in the middle. This will make it easier for him to raise a paw.
- Wait. Usually, your Rhodesian Ridgeback will sniff on your hand and as soon as he notices that he cannot get at the treat that way, he will lift his lightly-leaning paw to assist him.

- As soon as he so much as touches your hand with his paw, praise him, open your hand and allow him to take the treat.
- Repeat this exercise again and again.
- When it is working well and your Rhodesian Ridgeback lays his paw directly onto your closed fist, give him the command "paw".
- Repeat it over and over again.
- If this works too, use your second hand. Continue to hold the hand with the treat slightly off-centre of your Rhodesian Ridgeback. Hold the other hand open in front of the leg of the paw that you want (it should be the opposite side to the one with the treat in it).
- As soon as your Rhodesian Ridgeback lays his paw on your open hand, give him the command "paw" once again and give him his treat at the same time. If your Rhodesian Ridgeback looks at the closed fist, ignore his behaviour. Only react when he puts his paw on your open hand.

- Repeat this exercise again and again. At some point you can try not to use the hand with the treat but just to hold up an open hand as you give the command "paw". If he behaves correctly, praise him enthusiastically. If he does not react, perhaps it was too early and you need to repeat the exercise more times before you try it again.

Some Rhodesian Ridgebacks have problems at the beginning when their paws are touched. This is why it is not recommended to touch the paws of your Rhodesian Ridgeback and pick them up. He will learn the command this way as well and at the same time it is much more effective and agreeable for him to take the decision himself, when he is ready. You need to have patience and to give him the time he needs.

BEG

In addition to "paw", "beg" is also a very well-known command from the fun training sector. I recommend starting this exercise with adult dogs as it is stressful on the joints. Opinions are diverse on this subject, but you have nothing to lose if you wait a few months longer.

Now we come to building up the exercise:

- Give your Rhodesian Ridgeback the command "sit".
- When he is sitting, relaxed, in front of you, hold a treat close to your Rhodesian Ridgeback. Move it slowly upwards so that his nose also moves upwards. At the same time, move closer to him so that he does not jump.
- As soon as he slightly lifts both his front paws, praise him and give the treat.
- Repeat this exercise again and again.
- With time, increase the height of your hand. Be patient as, like us humans, for some dogs it is not easy to keep their

balance. However, with practice and repetition, any dog can do it.

- At the exact moment that your Rhodesian Ridgeback has reached the height that you want, start giving him the command "beg" and give him his treat.
- Repeat this exercise many times before you begin to cut down the use of the leading hand. You can pretend to hold a treat between your fingers after a while.
- At last, reward him only when he has reacted to your "beg" command without the use of a treat.

## SPIN (DANCING)

The exercise "spin" is easy to learn and looks very sweet.

This is how you do it:

- Your Rhodesian Ridgeback should stand in front of you to begin this exercise.
- Hold a treat between your fingers.
- Hold the treat a little over his head and provoke a circular motion from him so that he does a full circle.
- Reward him as soon as he has done a full turn.
- Repeat this exercise many times.
- Start to reduce the use of the treat and direct him only through your arm movement.
- When he can do this, use the command "spin" while he is turning.
- Now reduce the hand sign by making your circular movement ever smaller.

- Eventually, you can stop the circular hand movement altogether and just use the spoken command "spin". If your Rhodesian Ridgeback does not yet spin on your command, use the hand signal again and, after a while, try again without it.

## SHAME ON YOU

Now we come to one of my favourite commands: the command "shame on you". This is when your Rhodesian Ridgeback puts a paw on his nose or in front of his eyes as if he is ashamed.

You need a small aid for this command. I recommend a rubber hairband, a piece of Scotch tape or a small sticky note. It is possible that your Rhodesian Ridgeback does not react directly to the exercise with the aid you are using. If this is the case, try one of the other aids.

This is how you begin:

- Give your Rhodesian Ridgeback the command "lie down".
- When he is lying, relaxed, in front of you, stick a piece of Scotch tape or sticky note on his nose, or wind the rubber hairband around his nose. Make sure that whatever you use can be removed with one movement of his paw.
- Wait and see how your Rhodesian Ridgeback reacts. Dogs usually reach up to their

noses and paw the aid off. If your dog reacts like that, praise him and give him a treat. If he does not react like that, but looks expectantly at you, usually it is enough to wait a few seconds and he will raise his paw. If he still does not react, take the aid off and put it back on again. If this still does not help, I recommend changing the aid, for example, from Scotch tape to sticky note or rubber hairband.

- Repeat the exercise a few times.
- When he reacts reliably to the stimulus, you can begin to say the command "shame on you" when he raises his paw to his nose.
- Keep repeating this exercise.
- Then try to use only the command "shame on you" without any aid. If he rubs his paw over his nose, praise him enthusiastically and give him a treat. If he does not react, take a step back and try again later.

## BLOWING BUBBLES

"Blow bubbles" is one of funniest training commands, but also one that will cause the most mess in your house. With this exercise, your Rhodesian Ridgeback will learn to put his nose in his water bowl and blow bubbles. That may sound strange, but it is very entertaining.

This is how you train this fun exercise:

- Put a bowl of water in front of your Rhodesian Ridgeback. Take care that it is placed on a surface which does not matter if it gets wet, because it certainly will get wet with this exercise.
- Now wait for the reaction of your Rhodesian Ridgeback.
- If he puts his nose into the bowl, praise him and reward him. If he waits and does not react, you can intensify the exercise by putting a non-floating treat into the bowl. As soon as he fishes for the treat, praise him.

- If this works, reduce the praise. Now he will only be praised when he keeps his nose underwater for a few seconds. If he does not do that automatically, I recommend putting a few, non-floating treats into the bowl at the same time.
- As soon as he goes underwater, starts to breathe out and makes small water bubbles, praise him immediately and lavishly.
- Repeat this exercise a few times, then you can begin to use the command "blow bubbles".
- If he reliably reacts to the command, stop giving him the treats and just give him the spoken command "blow bubbles". If he does not directly react to this, repeat the previous exercise.

## CROSS PAWS

Crossing the paws is an exercise which I recommend particularly with female dogs. It would probably look strange on a male dog. The aim of the exercise is that your Rhodesian Ridgeback should, cross over her paws while in the lying position, which looks very lady-like. I recommend for this exercise that she already knows how to give her paw as this makes the following exercise much easier.

This is how you make a real lady out of your female Rhodesian Ridgeback.

- Give your Rhodesian Ridgeback the command "lie down".
- While she is lying in front of you, relaxed, crouch down stretch out a hand and give the command "paw".
- When your Rhodesian Ridgeback obeys and gives you her paw, praise her and repeat the exercise a few more times.
- With every repeat, move your empty hand closer towards the other paw until they are crossed over.

- The next time, pull your hand away quickly before she can put her paw in it. Once she lets her paw fall onto the other leg, thereby crossing her paws, praise her lavishly.
- Repeat this exercise a few times.
- Begin to introduce the command "How does the lady lie?" when she crosses her legs.
- Slowly reduce the help with your hand.
- Now just give the voice command "How does the lady lie?". If your Rhodesian Ridgeback crosses her front paws by herself, she has understood the exercise. If she does not, repeat the previous steps a few times.

BOW

"Bow" is another elegant exercise, but one which is suitable for male and female dogs. There are two ways to train your dog to do this. One is to wait until your Rhodesian Ridgeback stretches after he has been lying down and stretches, pointing his body downwards and his back half standing up, so that it looks as if he is bowing. This form of training takes a lot of time and you must always be watching to see when your dog stretches. Therefore, I recommend using the second variation which goes like this:

- Your Rhodesian Ridgeback is standing in front of you.
- You kneel down and hold a treat in front of you on the floor.
- Hold it so that your Rhodesian Ridgeback has to bend down to get it.
- Praise him when the front part of his body is fully lowered.

  Important: His back half must continue to be standing, he must not lower it. With the greatest of probability your Rhodesian Ridgeback will start the exercises many times by lying down. Use a second hand and pull his back half up. At the beginning this seems cumbersome but after a few repeats, your Rhodesian Ridgeback will understand that he should keep his back half standing up.

- When he is in the correct position, praise him and give him a treat.
- Repeat this exercise many times.
- Start using the command "bow" when he stays in the correct position.
- Now begin to reduce your hand signals and assistance.
- Finally, give him the command "bow" and do nothing. Repeat if your Rhodesian Ridgeback does not directly perform the exercise, and build it up again, using the hand. Try it again later.

## PLAY DEAD

"Play dead" is the last of my 8 fun commands. This is not the most difficult, but demands the most control from your dog. This is why I left it to the end. I have divided it into various levels of difficulty for you.

The aim of the exercise is that your dog should act "dead" when you give him the command "play dead".

This is how you build up the exercise:

- Give your Rhodesian Ridgeback the command "lie down".
- When he is lying in front of you, relaxed, get him to lie on his side with the help of a treat. As soon as he does that, give him a treat.
- That was the easy bit of the exercise.
- Now you add the progression that he must stay on his side for a longer period of time. He should only move again when you give him the sign that the exercise is finished.

- If he can do that well, start using the command "play dead" when your dog lies on his side.

  Important: Take care that he does not move, once he is lying on his side. That includes lifting his head or, much more difficult, without wagging his tail. Neither of these are wanted in this exercise.

- Increase the difficulty one more time by you standing up and ensuring that your Rhodesian Ridgeback stays lying down. If he is able to do that, then begin running back and forth and around him.

- If he is also able to do that, you can increase the difficulty even more. This time, you can start the exercise with your Rhodesian Ridgeback standing instead of lying. When he has also mastered this exercise, give him the command next time while calling him towards you. This means he has to carry out the command whilst coming towards you. Being successful in this step means that you have mastered the supreme discipline.

# - Chapter 7 -

# EXCURSUS: CLICKER TRAINING

## WHAT IS CLICKER TRAINING?

As you are interested in dog training, I assume, that you have already heard of clicker training. In the USA, it is widely spread and slowly, it is taking root in Europe. However, far fewer people know, what it is for and how it is most effectively used.

I am adding this short excurses to tell you what you need to know about "clicking" and give you a few introduction exercises, so that you are not among those, who do not know.

Contrary to what many people believe, this training is not an additional "click" to normal training. This is not, as many people firmly believe, just a question of clicking, when the correct command is carried out and then giving a treat. That is only a fraction of what is involved in clicker training.

It is more correct to imagine, that your Rhodesian Ridgeback becomes aware, that he has carried out the required action correctly, using a signal.

This assumption omits, that this is a completely different approach, which is based on trial and error. This means, in particular, that your dog will not be shown the correct behaviour by you, but always when he exhibits the required behaviour, this is marked firstly by clicking and followed up by treating.

Properly used, clicker training ensures, that your Rhodesian Ridgeback not only learns how to follow commands correctly, which is what happens in normal training, but that he will offer active involvement during his training. This way, he changes from a passive recipient of commands to an active participant.

If your four-legged friend is excited by this form of training, it means, that you can work on a completely new form of cooperation with him.

Clicker training originated from dolphin training and has since been used with a wide variety of animals. These include rats, birds, rabbits and even fish, wales and chinchillas. Although this kind of training is so successful, it is not magic. On the contrary, it is based on research which showed, that behaviour stems from its consequences. This means for you: If you reward positive behaviour, your Rhodesian Ridgeback will be eager to show the behaviour again.

Of course, there are those who insist, that it can also work with negative consequences. These people are not completely wrong. Studies show, however, that dogs, which are trained using violence, are no more obedient than others. This is mostly because violence causes negative stress and under such circumstances, dogs, like humans, are less able to learn. In addition, it can cause problematic behaviour, they are more timid and generally insecure in their demeanour.

You will discover much more about the advantages of clicker training in the next chapter.

# WHAT ARE THE ADVANTAGES?

In my opinion, clicker training has two decisive advantages. I have already mentioned the first in the previous chapter. It is the fact, that your Rhodesian Ridgeback will be stimulated to think for himself, and offer you several types of activity, when he is used to this type of training. This encourages him to use his intelligence in a completely different way than with other methods.

Apart from that, this type of training offers you another big advantage: If it is used correctly, new activities will be learned much more quickly by your dog than if you did not use the clicker. The unchanging sound of the click is recognised by your dog unbelievably quick as the sign of an impending reward. If timed well, this leads to significantly more effective training.

# FREQUENTLY ASKED QUESTIONS

On the following pages, I will answer the most frequently asked questions about clicker training as briefly and concisely as I can.

**What do you need for clicker training?**

The good thing about this training is, that you do not really need anything. Even the so-called clicker is not really necessary, because you could also click your tongue, make a beeping sound or something similar. Dolphins, where this training originates, are taught using a whistle.

However, for a beginner I would definitely recommend buying a commercially available clicker, which will only cost a few Dollars. In comparison to a word command, this has the following advantage: It always sounds the same. No emotion, no distraction or negative health impact has an influence on the tone. This is essential for the training.

**How does clicker training work?**

In order for clicker training to work with your Rhodesian Ridgeback, it is important that he associates a connection between the clicking sound and a positive experience, such as receiving a reward. I will explain later exactly how that works.

After that, it is always the same process, independent of how far on you are with the training:

1. You wait until your dog shows the required behaviour.
2. The correct behaviour is marked with a click.
3. Subsequently, the correct behaviour is rewarded with a treat.

**How do you get your dog to show the required behaviour?**

This question is the core of the training, because you actively do nothing. Your job is to wait until the correct behaviour occurs by itself. However, you can direct your dog towards the correct behaviour using clicks. I will show you how to do this in the section called "Introduction of the training methods".

**Do you always need the clicker and the treat?**

No. At the beginning you will need to click each time your dog shows the correct behaviour. However, once he has internalised the behaviour and carries it out correctly on command, you will no longer need the clicker.

The reward or treat that I mention above does not always have to be a food treat. Depending on the dog, it could also be a bout of petting or a game. You should reduce the amount of treating slowly once your Rhodesian Ridgeback has internalised the exercise.

**Which animals respond to clicker training?**

Every animal! It does not matter which breed. Age does not matter. You can try it with a puppy or even with a senior dog. Both will understand the exercise quickly and have fun doing it with you.

## INTRODUCTION OF THE TRAINING METHODS

TRAINING TIMING

As with most training which I have shown you in this book, clicker training depends on good timing. If you have never used a clicker before, I recommend practising its correct use before putting it into practice. As with the dog dangler, it would be advantageous to practise its use without your dog being present.

If you can get someone to help you, that is even better. The helper should hold a ball in his hand and you should hold the clicker. If you do not have a helper, you will need to do both parts. Now, concentrate completely on the ball. Your helper lets it fall, without warning, and you click exactly at the moment, that the ball reaches the ground. Repeat this a few times until your timing is perfect.

After that you can increase the difficulty. This time, let your helper throw the ball in the air instead of letting it fall. You should click when it reaches its highest point, not sooner and not later. Once your timing is perfect, you can start training with your dog, not before.

## BUILDING UP ASSOCIATIONS WITH THE CLICKER

Up to now, your dog has not formed any associations with the clicker, how could he? For him, it is a sound, like any other. Now we want to change that and you will be surprised how quickly it works.

For this training, you will need to keep the clicker and a reward ready. This could be a food treat but does not have to be. It is important, that it makes your dog happy and he wants to have more of it. For most beginners, food is the simplest alternative, that is why I will often refer to the food treat as the reward. You can interchange this with other forms of rewards as you wish.

Now we will begin with the classical conditioning. We want your Rhodesian Ridgeback to associate the click sound with a treat. This is how you do it:

1. Click once.
2. Immediately after the click, give your dog a treat.

Repeat this association between the click and the treat at least 20 times, even 30 times depending on the dog. Repeat the exercise on the following day. Most dogs will already have made the association. However, if he has not done so, repeat the exercise on the following day until you are sure, that you have been successful.

But how do you know, that the association is there?

In order to find that out, use your clicker once when you see that your dog is busy with something, like sniffing. If he reacts and looks at you attentively and expectantly, the association has been made successfully.

It is important that, once you have made that test, you do not use the clicker for anything else but to mark positive behaviour. Do not dilute the effects of the clicker by using it to call your dog to you or to gain his attention. Ensure that the clicker will be used, from now on, exclusively to mark correct behaviour.

Here are some tips, which I have for your first training unit:

- Click first then take the treat in your hand.
- Try to give him the treat directly after the click.
- Do not aim the click at your Rhodesian Ridgeback.

- Do not look him in the eyes.
- Do not speak a word during the whole exercise. Praise is more counterproductive during this phase of the exercise because you do not want to dilute the association he has made.

In the next chapter, you will discover how to carry on the training with the clicker with a simple exercise.

## STOP FEEDING

The 'stop feeding' exercise is a good start to make clear to your Rhodesian Ridgeback what your intentions are with clicker training. He should be concentrating less on the food but showing more interest in performing alternative behaviour.

It could be useful to have a helper with you for this exercise, too. If no one is available, you can substitute the helper's hand with a plastic cup under which you can hide the food.

Let us assume for this exercise, that someone is helping you. Give this person a few treats which he holds in a closed hand. Let him crouch down and stretch out both hands in front of him. Make your dog 'sit' in front of this person. You stand directly behind the person, so that you can see both his hands and your dog well.

Wait and watch your dog's behaviour. Instinctively he will be interested in the hand with the treats and will sniff at it thoroughly. However, that is not the point of this exercise. We want him to ignore the hand with the treats and touch the other hand with his nose. Only then do we click and give him a treat from the treats hand. At the beginning of your clicker training, your dog will not do this on his own, if he is not used to offering you a choice of actions. You will have to support him a little. That goes like this:

Let your helper keep his hands close together at first – about 8 inches apart. For the meantime, as soon as your dog stops sniffing at the treats hand for a brief moment and looks at the other hand, you can give him a click. If that goes well, you should stop the clicking because it is not enough for him to look only at the empty hand.

Your dog will probably be upset, because he is waiting for his reward. Wait and see what he does and reward him with a click when he makes a small move towards the other hand. It could take a while but at some point, he will do it correctly. Click and give him his reward. Repeat this exercise until it works well. Then comes the next stage of difficulty. He has to get even closer. When that too works, you can either ask him to get closer, or go directly to expecting him to touch the empty hand for the next click.

The biggest challenge in clicker training is not the timing, nor the waiting, but the silence. Perhaps you have noticed, that I have not suggested a command yet, and this is on purpose. During clicker training, very little is spoken. Only when your Rhodesian Ridgeback has performed the activity correctly and to your satisfaction, and you want him to repeat this later to a command, you can then begin to give the command at the same time as the click. Only then, and at no other time during the clicker training, should you speak - no praise and no talking in between.

I know how difficult that is at the beginning, but I can assure you from my own experience, that it is the most successful way of completing the exercise.

I recommend, that you keep the training sessions short at the beginning, so that your dog does not become too stressed. 10 to 15 clicks (including rewards) are enough. You can play with your Rhodesian Ridgeback afterwards or give him a hug. You can repeat this 3 to 5 times a day. Make sure, that your dog is mentally fit enough. If your dog is completely exhausted after training, which is entirely possible, let him have the rest of the day off; let him have a rest.

This is a hard challenge for dogs, which have always been used to paying attention to the food, but it is a good lesson. They learn that it can be equally gratifying to ignore the food and do something else instead.

## EXERCISING WITH THE CRATE

Now we will progress to something a little more difficult. The exercise with the crate is a classical form showing how you can continue with your clicker training. What do you need? Only a crate, a cardboard box or something with which your Rhodesian Ridgeback can interact.

Firstly, you put the crate in the room and reward your dog for everything which looks to you like an interaction with it. If your dog looks at the crate, click and reward. If he goes to the crate, click and reward. If he nudges the crate, click and reward etc. Encourage everything which has to do with the crate.

After that you can start requesting certain behaviour. Stop clicking for every other interaction and only click when he shows the behaviour you want.

As with the first exercise, some dogs will be upset when you stop clicking certain behaviour, which received clicks before. Generally, they start to show more of a new kind of behaviour.

What can you do if your dog does not participate and nothing works?

Firstly, it is important to know, that you are not alone. Particularly beginners in clicker training become very disappointed and quickly frustrated when their Rhodesian Ridgeback does not flash into action like a firework, but does nothing at all at the beginning. This is not the exception, rather it is the rule as he must learn that you will not give the signal for action but that he must become active.

You will help him, if you lower your expectations. This is a beginner's exercise and EVERY interaction will be rewarded, and that is a success on its own. Every little thing is wonderful and right. In addition, not only your Rhodesian Ridgeback must get used to it, but you too. You must get used to the timing and how the click and reward system works. Do not underestimate your own influence. Do not expect too much from either of you – after all, no one is born a master and, at the beginning, even the smallest success counts. With practice, you will become more confident and you will work well together as a team.

You can simplify this exercise by putting the crate directly next to him or hold it in front of his nose. If that does not help, then do not look at your dog, only at the crate. If you show him that it is exciting and interesting for you, your enthusiasm can often transfer over to your dog. Be careful, that you do not miss the moment when he looks at the crate. That is when he will be rewarded by you!

If you are getting the feeling, that your dog is afraid of the crate, or perhaps disturbed by something else, then change the object you are using and try some-thing else.

Finally, I have the following tip for you: Many dogs work better, if you start the exercise with a command. After that, they know that it is time to show their own initiative. For example, I usually start every clicker training with the command "showtime". After a few repetitions, your dog will learn what you are expecting from him and will offer you various alternatives.

In this training, also, it is important not to overstretch your Rhodesian Ridgeback, but to use the clicker often. I recommend a rate of 10 – 15 clicks per minute. At the beginning, one minute is enough. It is better to train for a shorter time but more often. It is also recommended, that you finish the training while your dog is still enthusiastic about it.

## MORE IDEAS

I hope that, in the previous pages, I was able to give you an idea of what clicker training is all about. Remember that, although you can introduce ideas, your Rhodesian Ridgeback must think of the idea by himself. You do not give any commands, but react on the actions of your dog. You can encourage him, by making smaller steps, but you should not do anything else.

Something you can also do, is to try training with a target stick. Naturally, you can buy these in the shops, but a fly swat or ordinary stick will do equally well. Make sure, that the end is well visible, for example by using a bright colour, and it should also be a little thicker, so that it does not accidentally land inside his nostrils. You could, as an example, put a small ball at the end of the stick.

Again here, before you start practising with your dog, you should practise holding the target stick and the clicker in one hand, so that the other one is free for the treats. As soon as you are sure how to handle it, hold the stick in front of your dog. As soon as he looks at it – as most dogs would – click and give him a reward. While you are giving him his treat, you should hold the stick behind your back. After that, bring it back to the front again and reward him every time he acknowledges the stick. Repeat this over and over again. Here, you should also pace the exercise at 10 – 15 clicks per minute.

If you are satisfied with that, stop rewarding him for just looking at it. Do not click again until he touches the stick with his nose. Your dog will not like that very much and he will try to show you his displeasure. Be ready to click at the tiniest touch of the stick with his nose, or if you prefer, you can build in a further stage, rewarding him for getting closer to it.

Once this exercise is working reliably, you can go to the next step. Hold the stick a little higher or lower. Let your dog stretch or crouch before he can touch the stick with his nose. Alternatively, you can hold it further away so that he has to walk a few steps. You can make him walk up a step or climb onto a stool. Do not click until he touches it with his nose. Be aware that success, in all the variations which I have mentioned above, is the result of countless hours of training.

If your dog is able to do all that, you can use your imagination to find new exercises. For example, do not click until your Rhodesian Ridgeback has walked a few steps with his nose on the stick. You can let him walk in a circle or practise with him walking "to heal".

Remember not to speak to him! However, if he has accomplished an exercise to your satisfaction, you can give him an extra command by speaking at the same time as you click.

After a while, you will see, if he reacts to only the spoken command. If he does, it means he has understood, if not take a step back and try again with the target stick and clicker.

Apart from the crate and stick, you can use any other object, which can cause an interaction. My secret tip is to go to a flea market where you can buy toys for small children. These are usually very cheap and robust and are excellent for your dog to poke his nose at, or roll, lift or otherwise move. You can use practically anything, a tumbler or even a child's piano. A toy car is excellent object to provoke spontaneous interaction, just as a ball or a hulahoop could be.

Try various things out to see how your Rhodesian Ridgeback reacts to the objects. You can decide in advance what you want your dog to do or you can develop the required behaviour as you go along.

Of course, you can carry out clicker training without any objects at all. Particularly by advanced training you can start with your clicker in the hand and a reward ready and call out "showtime". Wait and see if your Rhodesian Ridgeback is interested in taking part.

If you want to intensify your dog's behaviour, you can also use a clicker for that. For example, you can take the stretching game, which I explained earlier in the section for Fun Training, under the section Tricks.

If you know, that your dog likes to stretch after he has stood up, get your clicker ready and click regularly when he stretches after standing up. Soon, your dog will realise, that you like it when he stretches and you would like to see it more often. When he does, accompany the click with the command "bow". When he gets really good at that, you can try saying the command without using the clicker. If he reacts, he understood, if not, take a step back and continue clicking when he stretches after standing up and reinforce it with the spoken command "bow". Try saying only the command again after some more repetitions.

As you can see, there is no limit to what you and your Rhodesian Ridgeback can do. You can use the clicker to train all the tricks which you would normally teach your dog, although the process is different. Both methods are good and I would not describe one or the other as being better. It depends totally on what is fun for you both and which method suits you better.

# - Chapter 8 -

# SUMMARY OF TRAINING METHODS

On the following pages, I would like to leave you with a summary of the various aspects of dog training, which are important for your Rhodesian Ridgeback. Look at it as a kind of checklist, which you should work through to help your dog lead a satisfied and happy life. You will build up an intensive relationship and you will find yourself owning an all-round happy and well-trained dog.

On the next pages, you find the checklists:

- All about the foundation stones of dog training
- The best-known dog sports to develop the training of your Rhodesian Ridgeback.
- A summary of the most common mistakes and how to avoid them.

- At the end I will show you possible next steps to put what you have learned here into the best practice.

Go through the lists, point for point, to ensure, that you do not make any elementary mistakes.

## FOUNDATION STONES OF DOG TRAINING

In order to convey the training methods, which I have presented in this book, in an intelligible way and to achieve quick results in your training, it is imperative, that you use the correct methods. This is the only way your dog will understand what you want from him and be able to follow your instructions.

- **Loving consistency:** No matter what you try to train your dog to do, the key to success is the consequential consistency of the training (just like with children). Your Rhodesian Ridgeback must learn, that he has to follow your rules always and everywhere. For that you have to apply the rules consistently. If you sometimes allow him to do things and sometimes not, he will not be able to establish a link between his actions and your reactions. It will result in him testing his limits by letting his behaviour slide. Here, the rule is, to keep strictly to the rules throughout his life.

- ☐ **Positive reinforcement:** Always let your Rhodesian Ridgeback know, if he has done something good. You do not always have to give him a treat, particularly by commands which he has internalised, it is enough to give him a stroke or some praise. Positive reinforcement is the quickest and most sustainable method to teach your dog something. You should never work with negative reinforcement (with punishment). Dogs cannot understand that and they would be unable to make the correct links for any particular behaviour.

- ☐ **Your language and your voice:** Dogs do not understand the human language. They only recognise the sound of particular words and can link their previous experiences with it. That means, that it is useless to lecture a dog or speak to him in whole sentences. On the contrary, it makes it more difficult for him to understand what you want him to do and to carry out your instructions. If you want your Rhodesian Ridgeback to do something, give him short and clear commands. The fewer words you use, the better. If you want to gain his attention, it is helpful to speak in an excited voice. That will pique his interest.

- **Your body language:** If you want to make your commands easier to understand, or if the background noise makes it difficult to communicate, it can be helpful to use additional body language and to link it with your commands. As an example, you could link the command "sit" with showing an upright index finger. Over time, your Rhodesian Ridgeback will link both actions with the "sit" command and will also react when only one of them is shown. This also reduces the possibility that your dog does not hear the command properly and for that reason does not obey.
- **The timing must be right:** Timing is everything as far as dog training is concerned. It is the linkage between his action and

your reaction. As I mentioned before, there is only a short window in which you can reward your Rhodesian Ridgeback to ensure that the reward and the command are properly linked. If you are only one moment too early or too late, this could not only negate the effect of the exercise, but it could happen that your dog links something completely different with it, and it would take a long time to train him out of that link.

## TYPES OF DOG SPORTS

Apart from the dog games which I have already described in this book, there are naturally many other possibilities to occupy and stimulate your Rhodesian Ridgeback. There are competitions which you can take part in. You can train your dog for these competitions and allow your own competitive spirit to run wild. This type of training is a lot more detailed and time-consuming than normal dog training, so I will not go into long explanations of it in this book. There is a lot of good literature in the book shops. However, if you have the ambition to train further in this direction, it will serve to intensify your relationship with your dog. The following dog sports are the most common. Why do not you try them out?

- **Agility, Treibball and Lunge Training:** I have already described these sport forms briefly, so I will skip over them here.
- **Dog Dancing:** Here, your dog is taught a choreography of various tricks, commands and natural movements, which he will perform to music and which is carried out by you both. Your teamwork with

your dog is an important aspect of this sport. This is also suitable for older or less active dogs because of the wide range of movements and possibilities of the sport.

- **Obedience:** As the name "obedience" suggests, obeying commands is the core of this sport. Here, it is required that your Rhodesian Ridgeback performs your commands absolutely correct. It includes most basic commands but also precise retrieval over greater distances. The key to success here is good communication between you both. This dog sport belongs to the larger group of intelligence training and is therefore good for Rhodesian Ridgebacks, even those who are somewhat advanced in age.
- **Mantrailing:** The main task here is to track and follow clues. Your dog must find an artificial trail and follow it, on his own initiative, and at an even pace. There is a lot of nose-work involved. This trains both his intelligence and stamina at the

same time and is often used, as an example, in the training of rescue dogs.

- **Dog Frisbee:** This is based on the frisbee game. You throw the frisbee and your Rhodesian Ridgeback has to catch it in flight. In the sport itself, there are divisions between various disciplines. In one, for example, the frisbee has to fly as far as possible before it is caught; in others the frisbee has to be thrown and caught as quickly as possible within a specific period of time. There is also a division for the best choreography, the most tricks and spectacular jumps, and it is judged by a panel. This type of sport is most suitable for dogs with a lot of stamina, because their condition is strongly put to the test.

If the sports suggested above are not enough for you, there are additional possibilities for your Rhodesian Ridgeback, like rescue training and many others, which are less known, such as versatility training, dog gymnastics, dog biathlon, fly ball etc. With all training methods, you should ensure that your dog has enough rest periods to allow him to regenerate and relax.

## THINGS TO AVOID AT ALL COSTS

There are many pitfalls in the training of your Rhodesian Ridgeback, which you should avoid, at all costs. Failure to do so could result in you not achieving the progress you are looking for in your training and could become an unsolvable challenge. Try to avoid these mistakes in order to make it as easy as possible to achieve your common objective. I have listed the most common mistakes in the checklist below:

- ☐ **Confusing commands:** Always use the same command, do not talk in full sentences. Do not think of your dog as a conversational partner.
- ☐ **Wrong voice pitch:** Speak with an interesting and exciting voice in order to pique the interest of your dog. Rhodesian Ridgebacks can interpret voice pitch astonishingly well.
- ☐ **Missing body language:** Your voice and your body language have to say the same thing. If you are standing lackadaisically

and looking bored, you will reduce the probability that your dog will obey you.

- **Missing reward:** Always reward your dog if he does something good. Only then will he make the correct link and continue to renew that link. The reward does not always have to be a treat, later it is enough to give him a hug or simply praise him.
- **Negative confirmation:** Do not rant at your dog. He will not understand it and could make the wrong conclusions.
- **Violence:** It should really be obvious, but unfortunately it is repeatedly seen in practice: Violence is an absolute 'no go'! Training, using violence, can never be good for the dog and will not build up a relationship between you and your Rhodesian Ridgeback.
- **Lack of consistency:** Consistency is the key to success. You should enforce your rules without exception, even when it becomes tiring or when your dog is looking at you imploringly. Your training will not work

without consistency and your dog will not recognise you as the undisputed pack leader.

- ☐ **Lack of patience:** Sometimes it can take a long time until your dog has learned a new command or understood what he should do in a particular circumstance. Do not lose your patience! Just as a constant drip will wear away the stone, with enough repetition, at some point your Rhodesian Ridgeback will understand what you are trying to teach him.

- ☐ **Unfavourable timing:** Never forget, that it is a question of correct timing as to when you reward your dog. Otherwise you destroy any progress you think you may have made. It could be better not to reward him at all, than to reward him too late!

- ☐ **Wrong definition of roles:** Which of you is the pack leader? Who goes for a walk with whom? Who is training whom? If you are not sure which of you is the boss, then it is not you! If you are not the unmistakable pack leader, your Rhodesian Ridgeback will never follow you unconditionally.

- **Seeing dogs as people:** See your dog as what he is – a dog – and not a partner or child replacement. Find out what his needs are and do not place expectations on him which he cannot fulfil. Accept your Rhodesian Ridgeback as a dog with all his strengths and weaknesses.
- **Stop at the right time:** Finish your training session at the right time, even if your dog is not showing any signs of tiredness. If you overdo it, there is a danger of exciting him too much or putting too much mental strain on him. This can lead to him not being able to store the information, which led to the progress he achieved during his training. Finish each training session with a lot of petting and cuddling to give him a positive conclusion to his training.

# THE NEXT STEPS

It is important for you and your Rhodesian Ridgeback to put into practice what you have both learned. The next checklist will help you to get a good start and to put the theoretical knowledge you have gained quickly into practice. The following points are important to note:

- ☐ **A starting method:** Find a training method, which you have read about in the physical, intelligence or fun training section, which you think it is suitable for you and your dog to begin with.
- ☐ **Increasing the distraction:** Start every exercise inside the house, then change to your garden before you start training in a park or woods. In this way you can increase the number of things which could distract him slowly and it will not overtax your dog.
- ☐ **Slowly but surely:** If you are stuck on an exercise, go back a step and practise what you have already trained. Perhaps your Rhodesian Ridgeback has not internalised

the training as much as you thought he has done. If you need to, you can delay the training to a later time, it is possible, that your dog is physically or mentally exhausted.

- ☐ **Professional help:** If you fail continually to get any further with your training, or if there is a problem which you cannot solve and you are in danger of making it worse, you should contact a professional dog trainer or enrol at a dog school. Here you will get help quickly, or at least receive some good advice.
- ☐ **Optimise your methods:** Always second guess your training methods. Think about how your training is going and what you can perhaps improve upon, in order to strengthen the relationship between you and your Rhodesian Ridgeback and to accelerate your progress. No one is born a master!
- ☐ **Professional sport:** Once you have mostly put into practice the training methods which you have learned in this book, and

your dog has mastered them, you can think about taking the next step. If you are looking for a new challenge, you could take part in tournaments, measure yourselves with others and meet other enthusiasts.

- ☐ **Further literature:** If you want to get a deeper look into some of the subjects mentioned in this book, there are a lot of good, detailed books on the market which deal with a wide range of specific topics.

**The 72-hour rule:** Scientific studies have shown, that almost 99% of all plans and intentions, which you have not put into practice within the first 72 hours, will never be realised. I wholeheartedly agree, based on my experience. Therefore, you should start with the first training method within the next 72 hours, or at least initiate it. You do not have to do it perfectly, but it is important, that you have made a start, after which you can slowly improve on it, day after day.

# - Chapter 9 -

# CONCLUSION

Congratulations!

You have digested a large amount of knowledge with which you can improve your relationship with your Rhodesian Ridgeback. You are now in a position to tire him out physically and mentally, and you have also learned a few fun tricks.

You have now learned:

- What dog training is really about ...
- ... and why it is especially important and useful for your Rhodesian Ridgeback.
- You know the difference between physical and intelligence training.
- You know what is important in physical training and where your Rhodesian Ridgeback's abilities lie.

- You have received a step-by-step guide how to start teaching your dog retrieval skills and dog-dangler exercises.
- You know how to enhance his hunting instinct using these two skill sets, at the same time being able to keep him under control.
- In addition, you know other methods of training, such as agility, Treibball or lunge training. You also know that it is better to teach these skills under the watchful eye of a dog trainer and not try to do it alone.
- You have learned what intelligence training is all about and what advantages there are when your Rhodesian Ridgeback is trained to solve tasks on his own.
- You know how to carry out scent training and memory training, step-by-step, and know many further aspects of intelligence training.
- Finally, you have learned several exercises which are more for entertainment purposes but which will encourage and facilitate

your Rhodesian Ridgeback's powers of concentration.

This book has given you an overview as to how you turn your Rhodesian Ridgeback not only into a companion for life but also into a contributor and friend.

When you start integrating the methods in this book into your everyday life, you will notice how your relationship with your Rhodesian Ridgeback changes. You will pay more attention to each other and, in particular, your dog will become more even-tempered, because he is being trained according to the characteristics of his breed.

I wish you both much pleasure in discovering how you can develop your human-dog relationship, if you are willing to invest time and effort into it.

## BOOK RECOMMENDATION FOR YOU

**Get the first volume now and find out how to train your Rhodesian Ridgeback puppy.**

## Rhodesian Ridgeback Training – Dog Training for your Rhodesian Ridgeback puppy

The training of dogs is often...
»... confused with classical dog training drills.
»... only considered necessary for demanding dogs.
»... mocked by other dog owners.
»... replaced by anti-authoritarian methods.
»... considered too difficult to achieve without experience.

**What constitutes dog training and what is it good for? And how can you and your Rhodesian Ridgeback profit from it without having any experience?**

The most important thing is to understand how a dog sees his world, what is "normal" for him and how you can use this to your advantage. In addition, the characteristics of each breed are significant when you get beyond the basic training phase. Your Rhodesian Ridgeback will show characteristics which are different to those of a Pug, for example, and this is predominantly what you need to consider during training.

**Read about background information, read experience reports and obtain step-by-step instructions and secret tips which are tailor-made for your Rhodesian Ridgeback.**

**Get the third volume now and find out how to take care of your Rhodesian Ridgeback!**

**Rhodesian Ridgeback Training Vol 3 – Taking care of your Rhodesian Ridgeback**

**Taking care of a dog is often ...**

- ... underrated and regarded as being unnecessary.
- ... only related to the grooming of the fur.
- ... completely neglected by many owners.

**What is really important about the care of your Rhodesian Ridgeback and how do you feed him properly? How can you recognise diseases and parasites early and, if possible, even prevent them?**

If you want to know how and how often to check on your Rhodesian Ridgeback's eyes, ears, teeth, paws, fur and skin, this guidebook is exactly right for you. You will learn what to watch out for. You will also learn what to watch out for when you buy commercially prepared food and what the advantages and disadvantages are of the various alternative methods of feeding, such as home-cooked, BARF or vegetarian or vegan feeding.

**Read about background information, read reports on others' experiences and obtain step-by-step instructions and secret tips which are tailor-made for your Rhodesian Ridgeback.**

# DID YOU ENJOY MY BOOK?

Now you have read my book, you know how best to train your grown-up Rhodesian Ridgeback. This is why I am asking you now for a small favour. Customer reviews are an important part of every product offered by Amazon. It is the first thing that customers look at and, more often than not, is the main reason whether or not they decide to buy the product. Considering the endless number of products available at Amazon, this factor is becoming increasingly important.

If you liked my book, I would be more than grateful if you could leave your review by Amazon. How do you do that? Just click on the "Write a customer review"-button (as shown below), which you find on the Amazon product page of my book or your orders site:

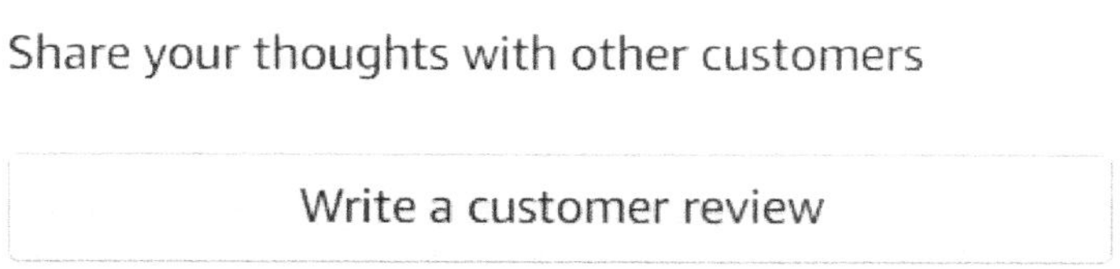

Just write a short review as to whether you particularly liked my book or if there is something I can improve on. It will not take more than 2 minutes, honestly!

Be assured, I will read every review personally. It will help me a lot to improve my books and to tailor them to your wishes.

For this I say to you:

# Thank you very much!

Yours
Claudia

# REFERENCES

Winkler, Sabine: So lernt mein Hund: Der Schlüssel für die erfolgreiche Erziehung und Ausbildung. 3. Auflage. Stuttgart: Kosmos Verlag

Obschernicat, Peter: Rhodesian Ridgeback – Charakter, Erziehung, Gesundheit. 1. Auflage. Schwarzenbeck: Cadmos Verlag 2015

Jansen, Karin: Rhodesian Ridgeback richtig verstehen – Zusammenleben, Erziehung & Beschäftigung. 1. Auflage. Hamburg: Diplomica Verlag 2013

Rütter, Martin; Buisman, Andrea: Hundetraining mit Martin Rütter. 2. Auflage. Stuttgart: Kosmos Verlag 2014

Fichtlmeier, Anton: Suchen und Apportieren: Denksport für Hunde. 1. Auflage. Stuttgart: Kosmos Verlag 2015

Schlegl-Kofler, Katharina: Apportieren: Das einzigartige Step-by-Step-Programm. 1. Auflage. München: Gräfe und Unzer Verlag 2018

Rütter, Martin; Buismann, Andrea: Hunde beschäftigen mit Martin Rütter: Spiele für jedes Mensch-Hund-Team. 1. Auflage. Stuttgart: Kosmos Verlag 2016

Theby, Viviane; Hares, Michaela: Das große Schnüffelbuch: Nasenspiele für Hunde (Das besondere Hundebuch). 2. Auflage. Nerdlen/Daun: Kynos Verlag 2011

# DISCLAIMER

©2020, Claudia Kaiser

1st Edition

All rights reserved. Reprinting, of all or part of this book, is not permitted. No part of this book may be reproduced or copied in any form or by any means without written permission from the author or publisher. Publisher: GbR, Martin Seidel und Corinna Krupp, Bachstraße 37, 53498 Bad Breisig, Germany, email: info@expertengruppeverlag.de, Cover photo: www.depositphoto.com. The information provided within this book is for general information purposes only. It does not represent any recommendation or application of the methods mentioned within. The information in this book does not purport to imply or guarantee its completeness, accuracy, or topicality. This book in no way replaces the competent recommendations of, or care given by, a dog school. The author and publisher do not assume and hereby disclaims any liability for damages or disruption caused by the use of the information given herein.

Printed in Great Britain
by Amazon

38423153R00101